Morphing into a Better World

Morphing into a Better World

Musings on Encounters, Connections, and Hope

Mark VanLaeys

In Loving Memory of my bride

mentor and soul mate

Emily Lissandrello VanLaeys

Acknowledgements

So many thanks to -

Emily, my wife who took a damaged vessel and over the course of decades literally loved the hell out of me.

My long-gone parents who gave a lot over the years, especially when I consider the burdens they carried.

Gay Brierley, my strongest cheerleader, for her love, insight, and unbridled enthusiasm which kept me on task.

Vera and her family for periodically checking in and reminding me in so many ways as to why I want to carry on.

Peter and Madeline who helped keep me occupied during some of my darker days with house projects and the consumption of lovingly prepared gustatory delights.

Nancy McLelland who loved me when I was the antithesis of my best self – and to her and Gay for sacrificing so much to make Emily's "Celebration of Life" a fitting remembrance.

Brian and Susan Anderson -wonderful friends– who shared their valuable input & gourmet food at so many junctures along the way.

Dan Syverson, my hanger-neighbor, author and friend, without whom I would have never even thought of writing this book. He was also my go-to guy who very generously shared his computer wizardry regarding the world of publishing and was greatly appreciated.

Dr James Lakso and Juniata College – who taught me via the written word and thoughtful prodding – how to look at life from another's perspective.

My extended family, UCC pew mates, the "gym Mary's," and other kind sorts who seemed to just come out of the woodwork when I needed them the most – Sharon K, Jenn H, and Breakaway Marc and Emily II.

And last, but certainly not least - Sharron Bassano and all the other kindred spirits on Substack who have repeatedly risen to the occasion to support me and my writing.

Preface

Ten years ago, I would never have imagined that I would be writing a book as the year 2025 draws to a close, especially one written without the loving mentorship of my wife. But life has a "funny" way of throwing us surprises.

* * *

Our world and this unique planet that we've been blessed with – are struggling. We have countless serious issues to address and existential threats hanging over our heads. Truth itself has taken a major hit, and "alternative facts" are as common as the rain. Words like collaboration, compromise, and civility have all but disappeared in many circles. And there's no letup in sight.

BUT . . . History is replete with examples of how the tides have changed when there are a critical number of people willing to confront the seawall.

The sense of *pervasive division* that is fostered by "news" commentators, talk shows and disseminated via social media is NOT the reality I've observed over the last half-century or even the past ten years.

That widespread perception, that we are terminally divided - is driven by the obscene levels of profit generated through the above endeavors. As we consume any of the above, the steady infusion of catecholamines generated (think fight or flight response) keeps us engaged, fear filled, and angry.

Obviously, there are millions of people high on that - fight or flight response, but they are in the minority at least here in the

United States. According to Gallup News, as of 10/25/23 - "Outside of presidential election years, between 30% and 35% of U.S. adults typically say they follow politics very closely." Those are the types of numbers that I've been seeing from multiple sources over the years. But keep in mind that not every one of them has swallowed the cool aid - be it red or blue.

As has become abundantly clear, regardless of which party prevails in American politics, the sense of division only deepens with each election, and each decade.

So, how do we change that tide? I suggest it is by making one connection at a time. What if we got to better understand those who are different from us? That is something that each of us can do!

I remember reading the words of a Jewish carpenter who lived a couple thousand years ago. He advocated loving our "neighbor" as we love ourselves. And that becomes so much easier when we acknowledge our common humanity. Recognizing and celebrating those ties that bind - has become my passion since my wife's departure for her "Great Adventure" March 3rd, 2025.

One could rightfully ask - "What would lead you to develop such an unusual passion," to which I would respond, there are two answers –

First, the short answer - I've met tens of thousands of people in hundreds of different settings and feel we're collectively better off when we take in the breadth of each other's stories.

Secondly, the following is a longer answer for those who would like to dig a little deeper into the origins of my perspectives.

I met my first barrage of random strangers right after graduating from college. With no healthy place to call home, I hitch-hiked through half of our states in a couple of large loops between New Jersey and California. I funded my travels via six short-term jobs which ranged from working in a Vietnamese refugee camp near San Diego, to pulling glass insulators off of telegraph poles in the Yuma Desert of Arizona

A year later, during my second season of tending bar in Yellowstone, I met, fell madly in love with, and then married a remarkable woman named Emily. After she finished graduate school in Boston, we moved south where I would attend the University of Alabama to become a physician assistant in 1980.

From there we moved to Tennessee where I worked for four orthopedic surgeons, and we had our first child Vera. Emily and I also went through training at a local university to become telephone crisis center counselors.

We subsequently moved to Upstate NY where we had our second child, Peter. And there we lived for 31 years. While there, I worked in Emergency Medicine and subsequently Family Practice. I did multiple types of mission trips which ranged from working as a PA in a Nicaraguan refugee camp during their civil war, to a multipurpose trip to Ethiopia in 2001.

The above is an abridged list of my employed work and volunteer efforts – all of which is to say that I've met and worked with an inordinately large number of people in all types of capacities. Some of these provided glimpses of people at their worst such as during my time working in the ER or as a Community Mediator.

And then there were also the joy-filled days where I got to see individuals with all types of disabilities - shine as they blew their way through the obstacles inherent to adaptive sports.

Through all of these, I've become convinced that regardless of the levels of gifts or abilities that we're endowed with, the strings that bind us together, and the values that we share, run deeper than the superficial differences that have been magnified with abandon.

As you read of my specific encounters turned connections, and the "musings" that help shape them, I believe you'll see how the tide of division can be slowed down, and with perseverance, even changed. It's easy to become discouraged, but please keep the faith. Life has a funny way of throwing all kinds of surprises at us.

Forward

"When two people from different worlds have a civil conversation about anything these days, it's a tiny step in the right direction. I suspect there are naysayers out there who would say, "Why bother, nothing's going to change?" To them I would answer, maybe not, but I don't think it's a waste of time, because people tend to listen to those who they respect. What if I turned out to be a different type of person than someone would have expected? What if, God forbid, someone turned out to be a different person than I had expected?"

- Mark VanLaeys

Writer Mark VanLaeys is a kind and insightful man, one who asks big questions that are of concern to all of us. He encourages us to take part in the dialogue and find answers together.

He asks his readers to consider, for example:

- *How can we, as individuals, deal effectively with the levels of division and animosity we experience in our everyday lives?*
- *When we encounter intolerance, extremism, or arrogance, what's the best path forward?*

- *How do we establish rapport with those who have completely opposing beliefs or opinions?*

- *How can we learn to really listen to someone who's extremely opinionated — and encourage them to listen to us?*

- *What is "engaged listening" and how can it turn differences of opinions into better understanding and therefore improved relationships?*

If these are question that concern you, I unreservedly recommend Mark VanLaeys' warm and highly readable book,

MORPHING INTO A BETTER WORLD
Musings on Encounters, Connections and Hope

Sharron Bassano -- Substack author of "Leaves"

View from my ultralight - "Aerie" – 2025 -Mark VanLaeys

New perspectives matter

Civilization has forever accepted the notion that a large portion of our relationships will just end up defaulting to "Us *against* Them" paradigms. But there is another option! We could prioritize getting to better understand those who are different than us.

Disclaimer

Making any effort to change the sense of division in this country, or world, may expose us to a wide range of unknown risks. The risks of doing nothing are already known and examples are readily accessible on virtually any screen, in any country and throughout every hour of every day.

Everything that we do in life is a risk versus benefit type proposition and each one of us has to decide which risks we're willing to accept as we protect either ourselves and the status quo, OR the lives of our children and future of this planet.

Regardless of the particular choices that each of us make, it is our own responsibility to proceed with caution and to use common sense.

Introduction

Most of the encounters and stories that I've included in this book have occurred over the last five to ten years. With three exceptions, they are all non-fiction, and they are shared with my full intention to stay with the facts as best I can recall. Many of them were previously published in my Substack Newsletter entitled "Us AND Them."

The names and some identifying features of the players have at times been changed to avoid betraying any trust as I retell their stories. Most of the photographs you see were taken by me, unless otherwise noted when taken by photographers from Unsplash. To them, I give credit and thanks.

The sequencing of the chapters was admittedly a challenge but was done with the expressed goal of enhancing the flow and minimizing confusion.

And lastly, I am a huge fan of metaphors and will add - unless you peel a few of the outer layers off an onion, you'll never get to the good stuff. In the following collection of my experiences, and musings, you'll hopefully agree there's a lot to chew on.

Thank you for being here and demonstrating an interest in - **Morphing into a BETTER World**

Table of Contents

Contents

CHAPTER 1

A Small Act Can Change Someone's World

Memorable days are like people. Sometimes they just seem so ordinary, at least to start with. A bit of ho hum, sprinkled with low expectations, and maybe even a dash of boredom as they present themselves. Such was the case a few summers ago. My wife Emily and I ate breakfast, then she shuffled some plants around the yard, and I doctored a few pieces of wood in the garage.

Photo by Mark VanLaeys – view from the Fine art and Music Festival

After lunch, we headed off to a nearby lake for the local Fine Art and Music Festival. The day was perfect with temps in the upper seventies and a nice gentle breeze. Scattered clouds and a remarkably blue sky mimicked those we would see depicted in some of the paintings and photographs of this lakeside village.

There were probably fifty or so canopied booths that weaved back and forth along the shoreline and a couple hundred folks - "Just Looking." A band comprised of musicians from Wisconsin and northern Illinois played an eclectic mix of music in the background. Nearby, a nice community playground kept some kids happy as their parents sat in chairs and listened.

Photo by Mark VanLaeys

We'd done a quick sweep through the rows of booths, bought some lemonade, and then went our separate ways to explore our notions of great artwork. It was an upscale event though I did hear a woman yelling something off in the distance and noticed a scruffy looking vender, who I'll just say didn't quite fit in with his refined appearing neighbors. His worn-out "GB Packers" cap did fit in with his mediocre quality woodworking.

I made my way down a few booths to an older gent, whose specialty was carving duck decoys of every variety that you might find here on Wisconsin waterways. We were talking as a thirtyish-year-old blond-haired woman walked by, calling for "Mallory," her step picking up as she went down the long aisle. By a minute or two later it was obvious that she'd passed a threshold and frantically ran by in the other direction screaming - "my daughters missing!"

Probably a dozen people fanned out in different directions. I headed to the water's edge, and seeing no one on the other side of the thick high grass, headed back up toward the playground on the one end of the town park. Seeing a young girl on a slide, I asked a guy, glued to his phone maybe thirty feet away, if that was his daughter. Though he seemed annoyed, he acknowledged it was.

I headed back in the other direction and while walking by, noticed the scruffy guy had walked toward the lake and was just staring. Not long after that, as the woman ran by yet one more time, he called out - "I think I might see a child in a blue boat on the end of that dock to the far right." The woman ran toward and past the "Private Property" gate and sprinted to the dock's end where she hopped into the blue boat.

As the girl stood up, dozens of people then watched her disappear - but only into some incredibly grateful arms.

CHAPTER 2

When is it OK to Give Up on a Fellow Human?

As we peer upon a struggling soul, none of us know whether we're witnessing the last of a dying ember, or the beginning of a bright flame.

Back in my days as an emergency room physician assistant, we had to answer the question - "When do we give up?" - all too often. When the heart of a patient ceased beating in any meaningful way, we would perform CPR, administer electric shocks, and then drugs, until an effective rhythm returned . . . or it didn't.

But it was never that simple.

While we were performing Cardio-pulmonary Resuscitation, we simultaneously had to discern – Had anybody checked for a "Do Not Resuscitate" order? "No bracelet, no necklace, no family - then continue." Protocols were adhered to, but every minute of inadequate brain perfusion translated to ever-increasing levels of permanent brain damage

So, with rare exceptions, it was complicated.

When it comes down to the unknown guy on the street or a struggling relative, deciding when to give up becomes even more challenging.

Throughout the 1990's, my main gig as a PA was in a small Family Practice clinic in upstate New York. It was twenty miles from the nearest sizable town. Our building was nestled behind Main Street and across the parking lot from the town's only grocery store and some marginally maintained apartments.

One afternoon I was the only provider working with a receptionist, a nurse, and a coding person on the main floor, and the administrator in the basement. I was trying to chart on my most recent patient, when I heard some very loud yelling off in the distance.

My office was right next to the back door. So as the yelling and screaming got progressively louder, I got up from my desk and had started walking toward the exit door when it burst open. A woman in her early twenties sprinted past me through the narrow hallway toward the right. Just a few seconds behind her was a man in hot pursuit.

Even as a slow reader, I was able to decipher the "F'CK YOU" in block letters tattooed across the front of his shaved head. Instinctively I did what I'd done hundreds of times before. I stepped in front of "my patient," extended my hand and grabbed his - though more aggressively than usual. "Hi, I'm Mark VanLaeys, a physician assistant - - can I help you?"

He wasn't in a chatty mood and within a very short time had broken free. But in that brief interval, my always dependable nurse had pulled through. She'd apparently had all but thrown his girlfriend down the stairs where she hid until the state police arrived about ten minutes later.

The next morning, I walked in the back door of the clinic as always. The receptionist came to my office - "Do you remember the guy last night?"

After acknowledging with a smile, she said, "He wants to talk to you." Knowing that my first patient was already in the room, I reluctantly asked her to "send him in." A minute later he came into my office with a baseball cap covering his mildly anti-social tattoo. This time he extended his arm across the desk to me. "I'm really sorry about what happened yesterday."

When the clock stops.

I walked over and closed the door behind him. He sat down and aired a long line of mistakes that he had made throughout his life. He was in his mid-twenties but had already spent years in prison for attempted murder. He was still on parole but shamefully admitted that he kept making bad choices.

He referenced the tattoo on his forehead and then lifted his tee shirt revealing a full-chest-sized swastika. He explained that yesterday's out-of-control argument was nothing new; it was just the freshest example of a life-long trend.

As I reflect on my two encounters above, I struggle to get past the enormous amounts of pain, guilt, and anger that were housed in such a brutalized young man. He was living proof that the effects of addictions, child abuse, and grossly inadequate parenting skills don't stop at the border between one generation and the next.

With enough of the right outside support, there would have been a fighting chance that he could have broken free from his past. But how many of us would have been able to if we had grown up under similar circumstances? This guy had built more roadblocks for himself than most of us encounter in a lifetime.

The overall trajectories that our lives take are determined by countless factors. Some are bestowed upon us and some we take on ourselves. In a perfect world, only the latter should be subject to our judgement. We've all made bad choices, but for a large portion of us, there were loving forces that kept the momentum of bad choices in check. My skinhead visitor had not been so blessed.

CHAPTER 3

Are We Zinging Right Past Divine Mystery?

GLIMPSES OF WONDER

My wife and I have walked along trails, mountains, meadows, and canyons for decades now. Our first date was to Jardine, Montana - an old mining, ghost town about eight miles north of where we both worked in Yellowstone National Park. I still remember so vividly the sun setting over the Gardner River, as it ran through the adjoining valley. Rumor has it that some rebellious youngsters from the east skinny dipped in these pristine waters.

As we traversed the valley and paths toward Jardine, I was exposed to the difference between my concept of hiking and Emily's. To this day, when we "hike," she's slowly taking in the moss, tiny flowers, mushrooms and moths around her, while I'm racing ahead, focused on the rocks, the roots, the birds above, and the destination. So many parallels could be drawn between our hiking styles and the way we travel through life - but I digress.

In my travels through a number of countries and a few continents, I have taken in the grandest of vistas. But I am still perpetually fascinated by the simple fact that anything exists. Anything at all!

Even one solitary drop of water - anywhere! That single drop consists of a billion molecules - each molecule comprised of two hydrogen atoms, and one oxygen atom. But where did that first intricately designed atom come from?

For those who would respond - "God made it," I have a small but related question I'd like to ask. Where did God come from? No disrespect intended, but I'm not going to start sleeping at night just because someone responds - "God created himself."

Is it too large a jump to also suggest that whoever or whatever created the first atom also created "HD1" the newest galaxy candidate which is 13.5 billion light years away? Or did it take teamwork to create the entire universe? This recent discovery by astronomers from the Harvard and Smithsonian Center for Astrophysics has me in awe over the unfathomable size of our greater neighborhood.

GIVE DIVINE MYSTERY A CHANCE
& STOP CALLING IT NAMES

Many of us, living today, were led to believe that God created all that is. Others of us were led to believe that Jehovah, Yahweh, Allah, Elohim, The Great Spirit, or other revered deities created all that is. In homage to Mr. Shakespeare, I'll just say "A rose by any other name would smell just as sweet."

So many beliefs regarding our Americanized God are inseparable from our culture and the agendas of our forefathers. But they're also entangled with the agendas of all too many leaders who wield

20

"God" as a tool or even a weapon. While religions are vulnerable to most of these hazards - I dare say that spirituality is not. The latter does not concentrate power. It lets people tap into the deep reservoirs and tributaries that connect us with something bigger than ourselves.

Organized religions, at least to my minimally studied mind, started out based on the teachings of well - intentioned prophets. Their guidance and depth of insight were passed on by word of mouth through countless generations and much of their tutelage still endures today because of the wisdom contained therein. Unfortunately, those teachings were also vulnerable to the translation and editing by fallible humans who had risen to power and acquired wealth which they desperately wanted to keep.

Remember what we saw with our own eyes on January 6, 2021, and juxtapose that with the revised versions that surfaced even one week later. My fear is that particularly in this post-truth era, many of us have thrown the baby out with the bathwater. The most bizarre and evil distortions of sacred truths should not take away from their inherent value or our sense of wonder.

Try to wrap your head around the fact that every single one of us is in the middle of nowhere on a tiny, beautiful rock, traveling at 67,000 miles an hour as we orbit the sun. Have we thought for more than a moment as to how and why our souls got here, or why we were even given breath.

Anne Lamott, author of Bird by Bird, put it so well - There are three essential prayers - "Help, Thanks, and WOW!" [1]

1) *Help Thanks WOW* by Anne Lamotte © 2012 Riverhead Books

_____

CHAPTER 4

Can We Agree that Actually Listening to Each Other Improves Relationships?

A Short Introduction to Active Listening,

Lessening the divide between Us AND Them requires at least a rudimentary understanding of "Them." And that understanding starts with some serious listening.

"Unlike most people, I not only think I'm right, I know I am. There's no reason for me to listen; since I'm at a point in life where I can just pass judgement and dispense wisdom. "

Disclaimer: I fully acknowledge that the last couple of sentences bear no resemblance to reality; however, my crappy listening skills at times might suggest that that arrogance is where I'm coming from.

A month ago, I had a phone conversation with someone I had not spoken to in a couple years. She made a comment which I completely disagreed with, so I let her have it, in a nice, "respectable" way. But even that is far from true.

Though I was feeling pretty good about myself for not raising my voice, an objective observer would have probably pointed out - that's merely a sign of basic civility, not necessarily respect. It was my words alone that did the most damage to effective communication.

I presented a short rundown of the many ways she was wrong, but my comments could have easily been interpreted as - "How could you possibly be so stupid, let me count the ways?"

In the end, I missed an opportunity to learn about where her comment and the underlying beliefs came from. Just as importantly, I missed an opportunity to reconnect with a decent woman, and a fascinating life. As it turned out, our conversation was relatively short and minimal reflection hollered - "What a shocker!"

Periodically, I'm reminded that I am not a great communicator. More times than not, that has its origins in my being a suboptimal listener. As I continue to grovel along in my attempts to improve those skills, I'd like to share the pearls that I uncover along the way.

Being a good listener starts with being *intentional.*

But I wasn't. I had heard her meaningless talking points before, so I was on autopilot.

Being a good listener also entails being *respectful.*

But I wasn't. How could I be, since I knew I was right. Unfortunately, I was right only through my set of experiences and filters.

Being a good listener requires being fully there and . . . (drum roll) . . .
actively listening!

At that moment, I saw no need to. However, in this troubled world, there's more demand for serious listening skills and growth - than ever. If my goals behind engaging in a conversation are to enlighten or convert, my next thought should be - get real and get humble. Those are the only ways to learn where another person is coming from. . . and it starts with listening.

CHAPTER 5

When is it OK to Laugh About Death

An all too true story

I would have never thought it was even remotely acceptable to laugh about the death of a single one of God's creatures. And yet, as I was recounting a sad story to my sister recently, she started laughing. To make matters worse, I found myself joining in.

I love flying and especially look up to all creatures that can take flight naturally and without things like Dacron and aluminum. On this particular day, I'd done the pre-flight on my ultralight and wheeled "Aerie" out of the hanger into a most beautiful and clear, summer day.

Having done a recent tune up, the engine quickly rattled to life, and I headed out to the west end of the runway. I radioed my whereabouts and intentions to any potential local traffic and was off. Everything was uneventful as I departed the airport pattern, but as I climbed through 2000 feet, I noticed a potentially lethal situation which I was not prepared for!

Photo by Mark VanLaeys

As you can see, there's only one seat here and it was that which I was strapped into as I noticed a second passenger - holding on for dear life!

The situation was dire because that little guy must have been holding onto the hairs of my thigh for several minutes and was surely exhausted. I thought about giving the fly a gentle nudge. But the propeller right behind us was spinning about forty times per second and would have created instant fly dust.

If I were Sully, who conducted flying safety seminars for years, I might have come up with some solution, but I didn't and by three thousand feet he was gone - one of life's regrets that I'll just have to learn to live with.

Oh, that they were all so small.

CHAPTER 6

Living the Good Moment

The Unacknowledged Agenda Behind Our Goals

Over the past couple years, I've often pondered the concept of "personal goals," and their place in my life, and in those near and dear to me. We've all chased them, and I trust you've seen some of the better ones through.

For me, an unmet goal has been to roll over the threshold that stands between a "recreational cyclist" and a "serious cyclist." Neither of these are an actual quantifiable thing, but that doesn't mean my head hasn't latched onto them. Like barnacles on an abandoned ship, I keep carrying around the goal - to pedal an old-fashioned bike a hundred miles in one day.

Literally thousands of people do it every year, so it couldn't be that big of a deal. It does take lots of training, especially since older muscles tend to whine considerably and even rebel when pushed unnaturally.

But why is it important to me? I don't know.

Maybe it's related to the fact that I was anything but athletic into my early twenties. I clearly admire the agility and strength of top-end athletes, but it's rarely the focus of my attention. Could it be that I'm hoping to somehow claim an inkling of athleticism? I suspect it's bigger than that.

Photo by Mark VL

Our goals may consume us, but do they improve us?

I was only four miles into a fifty miler when I noticed the sun breaking its way through some morning fog over a grove of trees. I felt compelled to stop and breathe it in, regardless of it being contrary to my training "schedule." My thoughts were racing in sync with my heart as I questioned - how many beautiful sights like this have I missed because of any day's agenda?

It was a short leap from there to seriously questioning my priorities in general, but specifically a relatively unimportant "century ride."

With every goal or aspiration that we lean into, there are opportunity costs that never quite make it into our calculations. As unique individuals, there are so many types of meaningful things that we miss while racing from accomplishment to accomplishment.

32

Goals can unfortunately cloud our vision as we look toward things that really matter - like relationships.

Understanding all of the above, this silly benchmark keeps nagging me anyway. I'm neither a psychologist nor an actor who's played one on TV, but I suspect that this goal has deeper roots than I recognize.

There's a lot of time to think on longer rides and maybe my soul just needs that. I've had a recurring thought recently. Once we're on a given track, it sure is hard to get off. Like a rabbit running down a railroad track, there's just no easy off ramp. Regardless of personal inconsistencies and the draw of common sense, momentum all too often wins the day.

If I can't understand how this works within me, how can I pretend to understand how it works in someone I've never met?

CHAPTER 7

Serendipity

In my last chapter - The Unacknowledged Agenda - I neglected to tell you about the most memorable part of my longer bicycle ride - breakfast at "The Main Street Family Diner" in small - town America.

As I was headed home, but still twenty miles out, my sniffer homed in on breakfast. I was cabling my bike to a sign, when an eightyish-year-old man trudged past, headed downtown. I said good morning but was not surprised when all I got was a mumble. He "sported" a three-wheeled walker, but ambled head down, with his eyes fixed ten feet in front of him. The cliche, "He looked like someone who'd just lost his best friend," came to mind all too quickly.

This wasn't the first time I suspected that advanced age had just wrung the last remnants of joy from someone - but it's always sad.

Less than ten minutes later, however, I was enjoying good coffee, an endless mound of hash-browned potatoes, perfectly burnt bacon, and eggs. The diner sat maybe forty people on a good day, but on this Monday, only a dozen.

I said hello to the guy at the table to my left, and we got to talking about life in this quaint town and where he'd left his mark a decade ago — cleaning up the area highways around the adjoining state park. He obviously enjoyed seeing us tourists liven up the town.

Our conversation was winding down when the guy with the walker I'd seen out front came in. He worked his way over to the table right next to mine. The very chipper waitress greeted him like all the other townies that occupied the place. And then as he sat down, she threw in - "Where's the Mrs.? " After a pregnant pause he responded - "She passed away on Thursday."

As she bent down and hugged this feeble man, he explained what happened four days earlier. Though he suggested that his loss was unexpected and tragic, he stated that she had already beaten the odds. That said, I so appreciated her kind, sympathetic arms being just where they needed to be.

Five minutes later as I got up to leave, I said - "Take care, sir," and this time his eyes met mine, as he said, "Thank you." This was certainly one of his worst days ever, but he'd fortunately had a place of comfort to go to. Beyond hugs and condolences, there' was so little that anyone could do.

I was glad that an out-of-towner at least thought to buy him breakfast.

CHAPTER 8

Dark Roast and Magic

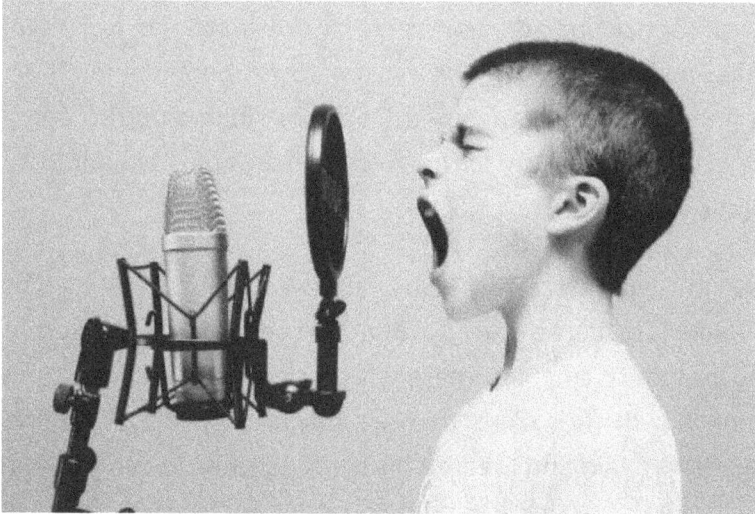

Photography by Jason Rosewell © - Unsplash

It's 2 AM, and my cup is full - not with coffee but with blessings (the java was consumed a few hours earlier while driving home from a concert). I had just slowly awakened to the song - "The Rebel Jesus" by Jackson Browne. It was running through my head, but I was stuck on the first line: "The streets are filled with laughter and light and the music of the season," but I just couldn't remember the word laughter. In my half-sleep, I kept wanting to insert the word Magic.

Back to last night - With my precious six-year-old granddaughter on my lap, and my wife Emily & daughter Vera to my left side, we were watching my nine-year-old grandson, Alex, on a Christmas stage with fifty other kids from his school. They're singing their hearts out. But he is not, and probably never will. He's on the Autism spectrum and non-verbal. We watch as he smiles and makes a slow turn to check out the voices behind him. Then, with his hand on his butt, he checks out the singers on the other side. The clarity and beauty of the voices surrounding him almost hurts, but it's therapeutic.

As my wife discretely dabs her eyes with a tissue, I see my daughter's loving arm wrap around her shoulder, and I silently pray. Not for him to sing, but merely for a sign that he can in some way connect with those kids that are having silly fun all around him. Alex turns again and I realize his pivot point hasn't changed in over five minutes and that's amazing progress for him. As the third song ends, the crowd goes wild, and Alex joyfully claps. My daughter comforts her mom with a smile, adding - "he's having a blast" - and it's true.

We eventually make our way to their van and then go back to their house. Alex runs into the dark to his frost-covered swing. Ten minutes later he joins us for a parting hug as we head out the back door. My bride and I walk slowly to the car parked out front. As I get in, I notice silhouettes. Alex and Vera are watching us from the front picture window. I wave like I have dozens of times over the years. I see Vera point to us as she waves. And for the first time ever, my much-loved grandson waved back!

Is it any wonder that I can't sleep and can only think of the word Magic?

CHAPTER 9

The Big Cleanse

Being of a certain age enables a person of means to undergo interesting experiences. For example, the character-building process of prepping for a screening colonoscopy.

Just for fun, let's pretend that a couple years ago I had to have such a test with its protracted fasting and then the grand flush. It's not a big stretch to imagine that I was just a little frustrated that people would eat in front of me when I could have nothing to eat or drink myself.

Then imagine that in the middle of this aberration (true story), I actually got a letter from the International Rescue Committee requesting money for the many millions of refugees around the world who lack things like clean drinking water, sanitation, food, and shelter, . . . places like crowded camps where hundreds of people can die per day!

I was humbled, as I had gotten only a fleeting glimpse of that which kills 494,683 children[2] alone in a typical year - and I had pulled out my "oh, poor me" card.

What does that say about me?

World Health Organization – Death from Diarrheal Diseases Newsroom Fact Sheet - published 3/7/2024

_____

CHAPTER 10

Kindness Plus Connection
Equals Gift

None of us knows when a garden-variety task is going to jump out of its well-worn path and become a memorable experience.

I had a wonderful day at the gym yesterday. The regular morning crowd was absent, and the place was empty, save for my wife and a young woman headed toward the back of the gym. Having seen her once or twice over the past couple months, I called a timid - "Hi." She responded with at least a hello, but I thought I might have even heard a soft - "How are you?"

About forty minutes later, I left the elliptical and headed toward one of my usual machines, but our fellow gym-ster was lifting weights nearby. I pointed to a bunch of weights and pulleys and asked, "Are you using this machine?" With the sweetest of smiles she responded, "Yes, but I'm on my last set."

Photography by Cayly Vanular © - Unsplash

It so happened that my wife was walking by at that moment, so I walked toward the attractive blond and said - "I think I've seen you here before — I'm Mark, and this is my wife, Emily." She put her hand out and graciously introduced herself. We did the usual chatter - Where are you from? How long have you been coming here, etc.

She was a local. As my wife returned to her workout, Logan described her boyfriend who usually came with her. I did think I vaguely remembered him. She had talked him into joining the gym this past summer and she was now working on her mom. And then, things got more serious

Logan, almost apologetically, offered that she was taking a year off after graduating from high school three months earlier. She slowly and intentionally explained that she was trying to find some "meaningful" work and that she didn't want to rush into massive amounts of debt. She then conceded that spending a lot of money was inevitable if she was going to get a good education, but her most pressing challenge was to figure out if that was worth the investment.

Then she methodically worked her way into her main priority - "I really want to raise my own kids . . . there's not going to be any outside daycare for them." During the ten or so minutes we talked, I said very little. As she ran through several career possibilities, I interjected that she might consider shadowing someone at least a couple of days before investing in her education or training.

With that sole exception, I just nodded in agreement, letting her tell her story. I never know in situations where I'm having a heart-to-heart conversation with someone, if I'm dragging them along or vice versa. In this case, there was no loss of eye contact, grabbing nearby weights, or awkward pauses. As for me, I just wanted to quit while I was ahead - all along savoring her trust, refreshing honesty, and genuine kindness.

My go-to assumption regarding eighteen year-olds, is that they tend to be a bit self-absorbed, short-sighted, and lack insight - kind of like me half a century ago.

CHAPTER 11

Salt of the Earth

I've always been curious and more than willing to learn about the different worlds that strangers live in. Each person has a unique story - and those stories fascinate me.

As I unravel tiny bits of what makes a person tick, I'm hopefully slower to judge and more likely to get a glimpse of the common threads that run just beneath the surface. Connecting in any way with that humanity gives me hope.

A Summer Bike Ride

As I pedaled along during this late June morning, I noticed that in every direction, miles of corn and soybean fields met the dense gray sky. A rare house, usually with an adjoining barn, broke up the landscape as did the occasional car, or rare tractor in a field.

This Hagie Sprayer can cover a swath 90 feet wide! Photo by MVL

Up ahead, however, was an unusual sight. A Hagie Sprayer was pulling away from a large tank truck, its huge tires carrying it above and between the rows of half-grown corn stalks.

Checking my rearview mirror, I started to pass the parked truck when I noticed the wave of an arm up above. I stopped, said hi, and then a fit-looking guy, maybe sixty, climbed down from the cab. With an outstretched hand and an unusual air of confidence, he introduced himself, and I followed suit. I started off by commenting to Dave that "in Upstate New York where I came from, sizable farms are a hundred acres. I'm still not used to seeing thousand-acre farms."

Acknowledging that I understood tractors have onboard GPS assistance, I asked a question I've been wondering about for years. "With farms this large, how do farmers know exactly where they sprayed an hour ago?"

Dave explained that the computer first generated a detailed image of each of his farm fields, and then it shades in the specific swath as his sprayer cruises along. I was awe struck at such slick technology.

He shared many different aspects of spraying the nitrogen solution. One thing he stressed early on, was the importance of keeping the nitrogen spray a safe distance from the local water table. They consider the moisture of the soil itself, the height of the corn plant, and when the next rain is expected. In this case, he lamented that the soil was particularly dry and that there was no rain in sight.

He was an enthused teacher, and I was eager to learn as much as I could about what goes into my "tank," or the tiny tank of my Prius.

Canadian wildfire smoke - Photo by Mark VanLaeys

And then Dave asked - "So what brought you to Wisconsin?"

I answered that our son had moved here for work more than a decade ago, and that our daughter had joined him shortly thereafter. Over the next few years, she and her then-husband contributed two grandkids to the mix - a now seven-year-old daughter, and a nine-year-old son, who is non-verbal and on the Autism Spectrum.

Then I explained that the critical factor which led to our moving west was that my daughter had struggled for years to keep her position as a school psychologist. It was impossible for her to do her best and meet the required workload, when she kept getting pulled from her job to address almost daily problems with her son.

We moved here in hopes that we might lighten her burden. Dave told me that he had friends with kids on the spectrum and had seen that their lives were far from easy.

While we were talking about other nearby roads and cycling, I received a couple different texts from my daughter. She explained that our grandson may not be able to continue attending the summer program for kids with disabilities, after all. The staff expressed serious concerns about his repeated and almost successful attempts to run off, despite locked doors and multiple aids on the lookout.

I apologized for being so rude as I looked down at my phone but then filled him in on the latest challenge that my daughter and her son were facing. His response was subdued but so telling. . . "and here I was worried about whether my fields would get enough rain in time."

We both had work to do and had already said our goodbyes when it occurred to me - this would be a story my readers might want me to share. I went back toward his truck, gave my elevator speech about "Us AND Them," and then voiced my observation that - "we've been talking for about half an hour and I have no idea what your politics are - and that's just fine."

He very aptly responded - "Oh, I don't mind telling you, I'm an American."

CHAPTER 12

When We've Seen One
We've Only Seen One

Does anyone like the idea of experiencing personal, reality-busting surprises? I don't see a lot of hands going up. We may like it when other people grow as we're turning the pages or sitting entranced in front of some screen. But more times than not, our minds are pretty settled. We know what we need to know, and everything fits at least loosely into our bone-encased narrative. So, there's no reason to shake things up, right?

The older I get, the more I think we may be missing some golden opportunities for enlightenment when we don't broaden our perspectives.

Photo by Mark VanLaeys - "Party Time" - Lancaster, PA - 2016

Years ago, as a relative newbie in the motorcycle world, I remember a sense of freedom as I worked my way from upstate New York toward the Florida Keys. On a long stretch through southern Georgia, the endless highway beckoned ahead, and all 50 horses of my Honda purred beneath me. Life was good, until it wasn't. My eyes started to burn as I passed one lush farm field after another.

The burning and tearing got progressively worse and I was having problems seeing - so I drifted onto the shoulder. As I lifted my leg off the bike, I heard a guy yelling - are you OK?

His Harley was parked maybe fifty feet behind me as he approached. He had seen me meandering and was hoping I would stop. After I explained what was going on, he turned, went back to his bike and rifled through his saddle bags. "Harry" returned with antihistamine eye drops because he'd apparently "been here" before.

Over the course of maybe fifteen minutes, we shared a few road thoughts until my eyes responded to the curbside treatment, and we were off on our separate ways.

But I remember his concern, and that kindness stayed with me.

There's a slightly strained relationship between Harley riders and all the other two-wheeled travelers - at least when pack-behavior kicks in. Think of "rice-burners" hanging from trees. If I asked you to describe the distinguishing features of a typical Harley rider, most northern Americans could oblige within a few seconds. Most of us knew "the look," and Harry had it. When asked to describe a typical Kawasaki or Honda motorcyclist, you might find yourself on a dead-end road.

Motorcycle aficionados don't drive Harley Davidsons because they're less expensive, burn less fuel, need less maintenance, or go faster than other bikes. Those would be the characteristics of Japanese bikes. A substantial number of Harley enthusiasts, at least to my biased mind, are drawn to the brand, its "uniforms" or clubs, or maybe as a means of belonging. There might even be a collective sense of machismo that rides along with the HD Logo.

What I've realized is that loyalty to almost any group entails putting on blinders which protect the member from alien thoughts or different ways of thinking. To be certain, some blinders are more opaque than others, but they're all key to the branding process.

The slow creep of blind loyalty to anything precludes considerations of the evolving costs of that loyalty, both literally and figuratively. As some "brands" morph into something that would have been categorically rejected at the onset, they are slowly rationalized for fewer and fewer defensible reasons. Please feel free to read all you want to into this paragraph – it is indeed a metaphor.

So, what do we do with "the Harry's" in the world?

How about we give them the benefit of the doubt. If we had had the same backgrounds and experiences as Harry did, would we be thinking or behaving the way we do today?

I have zero reason to believe that Harry was anything but a decent guy. I actually know nothing about him, though tattoos, beard, Southern accent and a gruff character make it all too easy to toss him into one of the larger baskets that I carry. Would we have agreed on most of the answers to life's biggest questions? Maybe. Would we have agreed on the best policy initiatives to address societal challenges? I doubt it.

Let's presume that there are millions of people who have been drawn onto chutes with no easy exit ramps. Be it problems with addiction, poverty, consumerism, homelessness, or misplaced loyalties, none of us are immune from taking that first step toward the greased slide.

CHAPTER 13

What if the World
Isn't Black and White?

A few years ago, my wife and I joined two friends at a local Mexican restaurant which had been acquired by an Indian entrepreneur. I had spoken with this fortyish-year-old man at some length, shortly after he opened it five months earlier. The small restaurant had previously been in the same family's hands for forty years, but the new owner shared his excited hopes for a somewhat different future.

As the four of us sat down we were served salsa and chips by the same Latino waitress, we'd seen half a dozen times over the years. Then we were each handed two menus representing the old and new cooks that were back in the kitchen. As we settled in, we watched the matriarch of the original Mexican family still setting tables and sweeping the floors.

As a couple of us ate our tortillas and beans, the other two ate aloo gobi masala. We talked about our families and recent discord that we'd either struggled with or danced around. Then the conversation drifted toward the many family skeletons that we so dutifully kept in our closets. In the process, I re-discovered that family dysfunction, including felony worthy behaviors, is not uncommon, even in the supposedly respectable white middle-class homes we'd grown up in.

Looking around at fellow diners and staff, I could only imagine the types of stories that they also could tell. I'm convinced that few, if any of us, live so-called normal lives. Maybe we should assume that other people carry as much baggage as we do. It may not be true, but it would give them a leg up - before our judgement kicks in.

CHAPTER 14

Revisiting the Past

A Mind Set in Concrete – Never Cures

Who wouldn't want to step back and enjoy one of their best days as a young child? Whether we remember any or not, we each had some relatively good days. Back then, life was simple. Soothing mother's voice is good, angry voice of a visitor, bad. Journey through birth canal terribly unsettling. First time nursing while being cuddled by mother - heavenly. Soiled diaper, downright shitty. Dry pull-up, a warm blankie, and adoring eyes of a father - all "swell" per the old black and white family TV shows.

Through the years, experiential learning expanded to things like screeching tires bad, piggyback ride good. Big growling dog scary, licking puppy wonderful. Nanna driving into the driveway good, police car driving into the same driveway after her, bad. And, we had to learn how to analyze information considering its source.

As we turned from little people to grown-ups, we either developed a little wisdom along the way or became particularly vulnerable to those with agendas that didn't include our welfare. I suspect that some people haven't worked their way through this stage of development as well as others.

Please step back with me again - All your fellow high school students and you just sat down in a classroom. It's Monday morning at 8:00 a.m. You're all braced to endure another boring class when the teacher plops down the dreaded - "pop-quiz." Is there anyone here who wouldn't have been elated to see that every question was - True or False?

Mere guessing would typically take everyone beyond the ultra-embarrassing fifty percent threshold. And lots of people at least in my school were perfectly OK with being correct even seventy percent of the time. Unfortunately, many people set extremely low bars for themselves, not just in school. When it comes to the big issues, like those involving relationships, our democracy, or even our planet, maybe learning the necessary facts is a worthwhile target.

On so many levels, we are all the same when it comes to dealing with complex issues or people. It is so convenient to lump concepts or people together - good idea, bad idea, good person, bad person, as opposed to thinking - maybe it depends. That person, after all, is way bigger than the matter in question. So many relationships and disputes have gone sour as we try to oversimplify that which is not even gray, let alone black and white.

We like to check boxes, almost like true/false quiz questions when we encounter issues of utmost importance. And once we've checked our boxes, it's like we've used permanent ink. Political parties, information on climate change, health care, abortion rights,

60

and gender issues are constantly evolving. Maybe the gravity of current circumstances warrant that we at least consider checking a different box here and there.

CHAPTER 15

Travels to Uncharted Territories

When it comes to reflecting on a lifetime of experiences, not one arrives in a vacuum. They're delivered in the context of other experiences - some related and some not. But the latter distinction hides behind the curtain of time.

Photography by Ivan Aleksic - Unsplash

I ask that you please pardon my indulgence into several chapters which revolve around my wife Emily – but she has done more to heal and reshape me than any human could ever ask for.

* * *

Back in the late 70's, I set off hitch-hiking from Aspen, Colorado where I had wintered as a ski bum, to Yellowstone National Park where I had worked the preceding summer and fall as a bartender. It was early May, and this time my destination was the Mammoth Hot Springs Hotel where I would become their new bartender and lounge manager.

The hotel rested peacefully five miles south of the northern entrance to the park. So, I pretty much had two million acres of paradise "beneath" me to explore.

I became a committed employee from 3:45 pm to midnight when the bar served our last drinks, but I spent most of my remaining hours on the trails throughout the northwestern part of the park. I would start hiking from the "Hot Springs" area in the early morning and head off in countless directions, savoring the best that this natural world has to offer. By early afternoon, I would head back to my cabin for a quick shower and then off to work.

Life was good! But I yearned to explore the other 95% of the park, and for that, I needed wheels.

So, early one day in July, I set off via thumb to Livingston, Montana to hunt for a used pick-up truck. The trek consisted of about a seventy-mile leg headed north on route 89 which dead-ended into an east-west highway that went a few miles east into town. The trip to the town must have been uneventful since I don't remember the rides or typically kind drivers who picked me up. I do remember traveling parallel to railroad tracks at a couple of points along the way.

After a few hours of searching in Livingston, I had prospects, but no wheels. With the summer sun above and the black pavement below, I put out my thumb as I started the few-mile trek headed west toward the road that would take me south to the park. In the midday, there was only a rare passing car, and I was starting to sweat more with each set of retreating taillights.

Within fifteen minutes, a very long freight train "ambled" by going westward, maybe a couple hundred yards away. I was the only one with keys to set up the bar, so I started running. By the time I reached the train, the best I could do was sprint alongside and lunge with one arm to grab a passing ladder. Winded, I climbed inside an empty boxcar and relaxed, savoring the passing fields and "Big Sky" vistas. The bliss lasted no more than ten minutes as the accelerating train passed a section of train tracks where I, for some reason, had assumed it would have veered left toward Yellowstone. But it didn't!

I quickly climbed over to the ladder, hung as low as I could, and dropped, hoping I could sprint and then slow down. With the train probably going close to twenty miles an hour, my dismount didn't go well. Though I can vividly remember going head over heels down the two-inch rocks, I doubt I've given the incident more than a fleeting thought for decades . . . until recently when I've reacquired that sense that I've just gotten onto a fast-moving train.

Before I fast-forward to 2024, let me say that a few weeks later I became the proud owner of a very used 1968, gold and white Chevy pick-up. And in that truck, I chauffeured Emily, a bright and caring young woman I'd just met, on our first date. We drove and then hiked to an abandoned ghost town and cemetery in Jardine, Montana.

As we sat among the overgrown grasses, wildflowers and surrounding tombstones of all shapes and sizes, we reflected on the passing of time and the hardships of those hearty American pioneers.

I'm not going to try to sum up the better part of five decades of shared experiences here, but I will say that Emily, and I have developed our own evolving perspective on all of the above. And recently, we've had a renewed interest in cemeteries.

Spring of 2024 arrived with an abundance of beautiful native plants in our small-town yard. All around us here in southeastern Wisconsin, the fields were coming alive as the winter wheat greened up, and budding soybeans and corn let their plans be known. As it turns out, new growth had been germinating within my bride as well.

During the first week of April, Emily developed some moderately severe symptoms that fit quite neatly into those of a specific and fairly common diagnosis. With appropriate treatment, she did not respond as expected, so her primary care doctor referred her for a CT scan. The reading of that one test took almost a week, which I, as a retired physician assistant, took as a bad sign.

My worst fears were greatly exceeded as we sat in front of her computer screen trying to take in the gravity of the radiologist's report. Though numerous malignant appearing lesions of many sizes were described, at no point were the number of tumors even suggested. Emily was confused and I was inwardly devastated.

Several days later, we sat down with an oncologist and his very proficient nurse-care coordinator. In my thirty-five-year career in medicine, I've met hundreds of providers, but only a handful in the league of these two. Dr "V" introduced himself as he shook my wife's hand with both of his, and then in turn mine, attentively searching our eyes. He placed his open laptop on the counter and then swiveled back around toward us on his stool.

His gaze now fixed on Emily, he said, "Please tell me about yourselves, I need to know who I'm working with." Though his waiting room was full, it was clear that he saw this as a critical part of his care for both of us. And then he listened, first to Emily and then to me, like our lives and futures depended on it.

After those few minutes, he took a breath and with a mix of compassion and conviction looked at Emily: "You have stage IV cancer." He went on to explain that there had already been an extensive spread of her cancer.

Even though it's now been more than a year since he showed us the CT images in his office, I can still remember the instant the diagnosis went from abstract to all too real.

Throughout our visit, Mel, his nurse, clicked away on her laptop, as the doctor outlined the many tests and procedures that he recommended before he would meet with a multidisciplinary team to discuss Emily's refined diagnosis and treatment options. By the end of the roughly half-hour visit, Mel read through the half dozen appointments and referrals she'd finagled on Emily's behalf.

I could not believe how quickly she managed to get access to such a high level of care - but I knew why.

From the beginning, Dr. V made it clear that a good quality of life was the target, but cancer care and research were constantly evolving. Elimination of every last cancer cell was unrealistic, but we were both encouraged that "years" were potentially on the table.

The physician's credentials and the reviews, which I had checked beforehand, reflected a learned professional driven by compassion, and a respect for evidence-based medicine. Those two exemplary human beings went further as they engendered a level of confidence and trust that I would never have even fathomed.

When we left the cancer center, we left with a bunch of appointments and the unexpected. And when you're stuck on a train that you can't get off, hope is a mighty fine companion.

CHAPTER 16

Going Head Over Heels
With Cancer

According to the American Cancer Society, there will be an anticipated 2,001,140 new cases of cancer here in the United States, during 2024. As I recently acknowledged, this abstract statistic has now come to life, as it includes my wife and soulmate.

To our surprise, we've encountered quite a steep learning curve. So, I'd like to share some of our observations and thoughts. They just might be helpful to someone down the road.

First, for a little context, neither Emily nor I were strangers to the ravages of cancer. We've both lost best friends to the disease, and my mother succumbed to its merciless tentacles before either of our grandchildren were born. It's just never been so up front and personal.

Photo Mark VL - Yellowstone back-country on one of our first dates

THINGS THAT JUST WEREN'T ON OUR RADAR

No two cancer experiences are the same

This observation cannot be overstated! My wife was told within five minutes of meeting her oncologist that "you have stage 4 cancer." Translation: the cancer is widely metastasized and not likely to ever go away. Some people may not hear those words for many years after their diagnosis, if at all. That might sound bad, but having been in medicine for more than three decades, I must clarify with a tiny bit of medical parlance - "It really sucks!"

There is such a broad spectrum of ways in which cancer can first reveal itself. For some it might be a suspicious looking, small mass on an x-ray. For a small percentage of "special" people, such as my wife, there's more of a barrage of nastiness.

As her husband, I'm not going to downplay the CT visual or the gravity of her physician's confirmation of the extent of her disease. I am saying that all things considered, we're grateful for every day that she gets to enjoy. We have a strong marriage and an honest relationship that has weathered some tough tides, but this is more like your "hundred-year storm."

Emily, over a lifetime, has developed a remarkable level of spirituality which certainly softens her response to this unpleasant news.

It also translates to heightened resilience, optimism, and tolerance regarding the ever-present unknowns of her situation. In no way should this suggest that she isn't committed to doing whatever she can do to "stay here" for all of her loved ones. She is just more at peace than others might be in her situation.

EARLY ON, THE UNKNOWNS ARE EVERYWHERE.

What is it? Where is it? How bad is? What's the next test and how soon can we get it . . . and the results? Who should we tell since there are so many questions for which the only appropriate answer is - "We don't know?" It's only natural to want to share such news with loved ones, but during the first couple weeks the recurrent barrages of unanswerable questions had us reassessing the benefits of waiting to inform the key players in our lives.

At least in our case, there was a frenzied effort on the part of her healthcare team to get tests and results as soon as possible because Emily was obviously way behind the eight-ball. We're deeply grateful for all their expediency, but almost daily out-of-town appointments, tests, scans, biopsies or procedures over three weeks left no time for processing, not to mention the typical day-to-day stuff that rolls by like a tank.

Time to merely sit down in a lawn chair, with or without a beer, became a luxury.

AND THEN, THE EVER SO HUMAN – WHY ME?

Though Emily and I briefly entertained that question (LOL), we quickly came to an agreement that the more relevant question might be - "Why not me?"

Chronic irritants, and toxic chemicals of countless varieties are frequently suspect regarding cell mutations, and we're exposed to dozens if not hundreds of them every day. Take a close look at the pollutants in our drinking water, the long list of chemicals in a random box of anything off a grocery store shelf, or the composition of the particulate matter that drifts in from raging forest fires. How many carcinogens are we subjected to on a regular basis? A dozen parts per million might be all that it takes to rattle our cellular status quo.

Living a healthier lifestyle, picking cancer "resistant" parents, eating a plant-based diet, getting regular age-appropriate exercise, and the maintenance of an ideal weight all seem to increase the odds of living a longer life, but there are no guarantees. Emily did - all of the above .

Life is indeed a crap shoot. Though we agree that getting the odds in our favor is a worthwhile goal, we were reminded that we shouldn't bet the farm on anything.

EVERYONE WOULD APPROACH THESE CHALLENGES DIFFERENTLY – AND THAT'S FINE.

Not surprisingly, we've occasionally received unsolicited advice from *well-intentioned* acquaintances. I make the distinction because people who know and respect us typically have a fairly good understanding of our skill sets, priorities, and values. An example would be our reverence for evidence-based medicine.

We also acknowledge that sometimes there just aren't any good options, but playing games with an aggressive monster rarely ends well.

Emily and I are both on the same page that the degree to which any patient wants to "fight" cancer is very much a personal issue based on their specific variables and priorities.

Photo by Mark VL

Kindnesses expressed were like a gentle rain on parched ground

As I was typing this, I was pleased to be "interrupted" by a friend from church "just" checking in.　　　We really appreciate the friends, neighbors, relatives and family who push past the awkwardness to just see how we're doing or send messages of support. Each effort lightens our load a tiny bit and nourishes us as we strive to set a different kind of roots.

AND SO MANY PEOPLE HAVE IT WORSE

We've been blessed to have each other, a loving family and a mostly supportive extended family, a roof over our heads, and a committed and compassionate care team. So many people with a new cancer diagnosis are not so fortunate. They may not be in a position where they can dig into retirement savings to whittle away at the endless medical bills.

Most importantly, we've been particularly grateful that Emily has been feeling well enough that she can continue to enhance her native plant and pollinator gardens.

And we're paying more than lip service to the concept of - living one day at a time.

CHAPTER 17

The Empty Page

Photography by Darren Lawrence - Unsplash

Staring at me like a caged, wounded animal,

    is a plain white sheet of paper.

This could go absolutely anywhere - I get to decide.

    I'm the guard of that cage.

For better or worse, I am the only one who has the key.

    I could start the process of healing, but

    what about all the wounds I already carry?

Do there have to be more?

Every day the fresh empty page beckons me to act.

    As if standing on some cliff's edge,

    It terrifies me, it seduces me. . .

    to tell a different story.

More accurately,

    to write a different story,

     until one day, I can't.

CHAPTER 18

I'm Sorry, I Was Wrong

Maybe it's just me, but it sure seems that there are a lot of us who REALLY struggle with the concept of apologizing. And right up there, in terms of difficulty, is admitting, "I was wrong."

I "lovingly" recall a visit with my father decades ago. We were talking about something, no doubt heated, and the conversation found us walking through his stuffed garage. There was a narrow path between a bunch of boxes on the right side and lumber stacked to the ceiling on the left. As he weaved his way down the center, I asked: "Don't you think you could stuff a few more 2 by 8's up there?"

My father was an engineer by trade, and he knew tons about things like live loads, dead loads and material strength - but there must have been five hundred pounds of wood above him.

He started to say something like, "it can handle it . . ." as he reached up and gave the center support a jar. Within a second, all three supports had broken or pulled out of the wall and the load came straight down. My father, without turning, dove straight backwards and landed on a bunch of boxes -amazingly not getting injured by a single board. He could have easily been killed but all he did was move a bunch of boards that had grazed him and kept talking as we left the garage - continuing the conversation. That was my father!

He never said anything about being wrong or stupid. If over the course of our lives together he ever admitted he was wrong or sorry, I certainly don't remember it. He was admittedly strong-willed and always had "good reasons" for why he wouldn't budge from his positions - just like other members of my family and those I've met over the years.

I screw up almost daily and have frequently admitted that I was wrong - maybe just to lighten my load of guilt. My wife of four decades is the same. Admitting that we're wrong hasn't killed either of us yet - but we're young, there's still time.

COMPROMISE –A FOUR LETTER WORD

Another memorable incident took place in February 2009. My wife and I drove from upstate NY to Florida to visit my 85-year-old father and his lady friend "Dolores" Their relationship was floundering, and he had recently gotten his own place. After visiting a couple of days, it somehow leaked out that I had voted for Obama, which was unthinkable to him, an extremely conservative Navy veteran.

My father turned quiet as we ate breakfast. I vaguely remember all of us walking on the beach in the afternoon but between the weather being in the 30's and my father not talking, it was bitter.

As dinner rolled around, Dolores directed the conversation to me - "You and Emily have been married quite a long time and seem to do pretty well working through your differences... do you have any advice for us since we're not doing so well?" I thought for a second or two and responded, "I think what's helped us more than anything is learning how to compromise."

Well, the man who hadn't said squat in the last five hours, exploded! His face turned red, and as he started yelling, his face went deep purple. I was terrified that this guy who I loved and respected was going to die right there on the spot. The last thing I remember him yelling was - "You're the most unpatriotic person I have ever known." After throwing the greatest insult he could imagine, he left the table.

Maybe an hour later he led me toward the bathroom and said - "I want to show you something." His color had cooled. I had just closed the door behind me as he reached under the sink and pulled out his 22-magnum pistol. With shaking hands and no words, he loaded the pistol in front of me. He hesitated. And then he put it back under the sink. I have no idea why I didn't just grab his gun - maybe out of some warped sense of respect?

My wife and I "slept" with a dresser in front of the door of our bedroom that night and left as the sun rose the next morning.

My father never did say he was sorry.

We talked a few times over the next couple of years, and he never again brought up politics. The following year, at age 86, he drove his well-used Toyota up to NY so our son could have it for his senior year of college and beyond. The following year he treated my siblings, Emily, and me to a wonderful cruise in the Caribbean. That to him was much easier than apologizing.

CHAPTER 19

Sweeping Generalizations - the Nukes of Destructive Language

I'm really trying to steer away from politics, but I can't intentionally steer away from reality. Doing so is destructive to the human mind whether it's via mental illness, drugs, or propaganda. When a nation starts to deny reality, it undermines its own existence. Our country has devolved to the point where we're struggling to agree on even the most basic facts.

In 2023, we can't even all agree that what we witnessed on television the day of January 6th, 2021, was a domestic attack on the United States government and democracy itself. A large portion of Americans refuse to acknowledge how serious it was or that we should do everything in our power to minimize the chances that it ever happens again. As pathetic as all of that is, it is the reality we must work with.

SO, WHAT CAN WE AGREE ON?

First, for perspective, please step back with me. Imagine, it's twenty years ago, and you're one of a thousand people sitting in an auditorium. The key address is entitled: "What America Needs." The speaker starts out by asking: "How many of you here in this room would agree that the indiscriminate killing of large numbers of innocent people is a very bad thing? Can I see a show of hands?"

I ask my current readers - is it a stretch to guess - a solid majority of hands would have gone up quickly? Maybe a hundred people would have been paralyzed by indecision, thinking it's a loaded question.

Now imagine that the speaker asked a very similar question. "How many of you here in this room would agree that the indiscriminate maligning of innocent people is a very bad thing?" My hunch is that a majority of hands would have gone up in agreement then also, though I suspect there might have been a little less of a consensus.

Now imagine *if the same two questions were being asked today.* I 'm not certain that we would get a clear consensus on either question. As a society, we seem to have an ever-increasing tolerance for amoral behavior when the conditions "warrant."

Making sweeping generalizations and assumptions about people, whom we know very little about, is indiscriminately maligning them.   Losing the awareness that we're doing so is a key step toward turning a stranger into an adversary. And that is a slippery slope with frequently unintended consequences.

A few days ago, I wandered onto a very conservative Substack newsletter from a guy with some credentials. As is sometimes the case, I found myself uncomfortable reading views that articulately challenged my own. The article in this case was so philosophical, esoteric, and linguistically nuanced that I dared not make my comments directly to this Harvard alum, knowing he could clearly -out-BS me.

So, I made comments to some of the people writing commentary - including "KG." We commented back and forth about the article, but more importantly from my perspective - about the generalizations she had made. I explained that all liberals aren't the same, any more than all conservatives are . . . we are each very complex. She defended her generalizations since they were "from my experience" even though she hadn't originally acknowledged that.

Over the course of six posts, the tone went from antagonistic to what I consider encouraging. Her last post ended with: "I agree as a society it seems we (L and R) have lost the art of true and civil debate, genuine concern for the COMMON good, and the ability to engage in true compromise on serious issues."

My final response was that I concurred with what she wrote, with one caveat - "I think we just had a brief, true and civil debate." Who knows what might happen if we put aside assumptions, sweeping generalizations, and rhetoric to make room for conversation?

CHAPTER 20

Why are We So Uncomfortable with Gray?

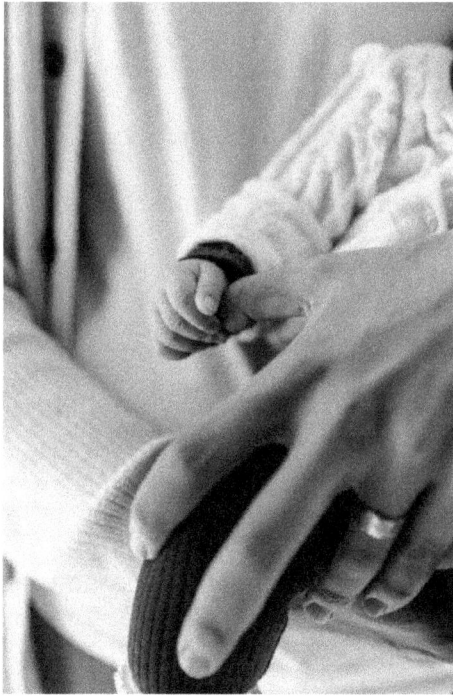

Photography by Nathan Dumlao © Unsplash

"Black" and "white" are simple,

    but they typically betray reality.

Though I supposedly am one,

    I've never actually met a white person.

    I've never met a black person.

    I've never met a red or a brown person.

Labels are quick and easy but so rarely helpful

    unless our intent is to divide.

I've never seen a pitch-black sky

    Though I have been dazzled by pure white, fresh fallen
snow.

I have never met a perfect person,

    though I have seen flawless flowers and trees

I've not yet learned how to pick them apart

    or label them,

    as I have humans.

That I was taught at a young age.

CHAPTER 21

Was I Just Spared Again?

I remember so clearly my sense of relief. It was mid-afternoon as I rode my mountain bike up the second half of a driveway next to a tall, tan, brick house. Though my mind at that time seemed like a blank slate, I had a sneaking suspicion that this house was the one - the home we'd been living in for five years. Progressively thinking I'd found it; I walked into the fenced back yard and took in my wife's many gardens. And then I saw her and our eight-year-old granddaughter "Belle" in their fairy-themed garden.

Emily, seeing that I looked confused, and flustered, asked if I was alright, to which I could only respond - "I don't know where my bike goes!" As she approached, pointing to the garden shed, I answered –"There's a crack in my helmet, I think I must have had an accident."

Then I continued to try to orient myself – "What is Belle doing here? I don't know why you're here, but I'm glad you are!" As Emily briefly explained that we'd ALL spent the morning together playing miniature golf, she led me into the house and said – "we have to go to the hospital." I agreed and surprisingly thought of the need to get my wallet. However, I had no idea where it would be. As I stood at the base of our staircase, Emily suggested "it's probably on your dresser." But I had no idea where our bedroom was. Belle took charge with her sweet "follow me."

After grabbing my wallet, I washed some blood and dirt off the back of my shoulder and elbow so I could sit in the car. Emily was "happy to drive" since I apparently didn't look up to the task. I noticed a large number of political signs on the way and asked who the president was, since the cooler day suggested it might be November. To add to my confusion, she knew a surprisingly large amount about the ongoing changes to the out-of-town hospital, as we approached.

Apparently, the ER staff agreed with my hunch that I'd had a head injury, as they whisked Emily and Belle to the waiting room and had me back for x-rays and CT scans within minutes. My memory was very patchy at best, but it seemed like time raced by. Though nurses and doctors were coming and going, it was during a lull in traffic, when my eyes were closed, that I got an isolated snapshot of a key memory.

There it was, a deep ditch crossing the trail a few feet in front of my skidding, locked tires. Absolutely nothing before, and nothing after. To this day, I have zero recollection of anything that happened over the miles before or after this ditch - until I just "appeared" halfway up my driveway.

I don't know if or how I negotiated the traffic at the half dozen stop signs or traffic light before I eventually crossed the main drag which leads to our house.

For several hours I'd completely forgotten that my wife had Stage IV cancer.

Putting it all Together

Between that fleeting image, my cracked helmet, and the deep scrape on the back of my shoulder, I've deduced that I probably did a three-quarter flip after my front tire dropped into the rut - landing me on the rocky road. This old guy could have gotten seriously hurt, but I apparently rode off into the sunset with minor injuries. It's not that I'm a tough dude; I'm not. I've demonstrated countless times that I break when I fall from heights or encounter immovable objects like trees.

Could it be that, once again, I was spared?

Three different times over the course of my life I've escaped serious injury when all the laws of physics screamed - "not this time."

How many of us can tell similar tales of woe? I don't think I'm alone here. At this point in my life, however, my wife and family needed me more than ever and I'm extremely grateful that I was able to carry on.

But there are innumerable cases of critical care givers being taken out of service in great times of need. Why am I still sitting here with merely a protracted headache?

Some people might say that I'm just lucky. Others might reassure me "God intervened." Others, would suggest, "it's your guardian angel." And to each one of them, I say, you may be right.

But in the still and deepest quiet, I merely say a most hearty thank you and slide over to make a little more room for divine mystery.

CHAPTER 22

A Tiny Glimpse of a Bigger Picture

Hopefully everyone gets at least an occasional, fine moment where they've sensed a connection with a force or spirit beyond comprehension.

One pristine summer day, maybe fifteen years ago, I was headed from the mountains of Upstate New York to Wrightsville Beach in Virginia. I was riding my newly acquired, 600 cc Honda Shadow. It was pretty much a toy version of a Harley Davidson Sportster, having only a top speed of eighty in a racing tuck.

I had worked my way from country roads to the eight-lane beltway around Annapolis. My throttle was wide open, I 'd become hopelessly lost, and was frequently tail-gated or surrounded by tractor trailers. I could be cool and suggest it was just a hassle, but I truly thought I was going to die right there - my legacy being an unrecognizable splat in the highway. To my great relief, the traffic eventually thinned, and I triumphantly exited at the first rest area I could find.

As I relaxed my derriere on the wide supportive surface of a picnic table, a couple in their upper fifties were walking by, talking in hushed tones. I asked them - "How are you folks doing on such a beautiful day?" Though they gave a positive response such as "We're fine, how are you," their tone and expressions betrayed them as they looked at each other. I'm uncertain as to where my gutsy response came from, but it was something to the effect - "I'm not sure I'm convinced."

They walked toward me as I stood up. Over the next twenty or so minutes they unpacked the many burdens they were carrying concerning their daughter, in her mid-twenties. I don't remember the details, but substance abuse and mental illness were featured in the ongoing nightmare that they described. I listened as they shared the many dead ends that they had encountered.

Their story was heart-breaking, but the despair they initially emanated lessened as their emotions were unleashed. We eventually hugged each other and they parted.

I then pulled out my map to try to figure out where I was, and how to get back on track. But I couldn't help but wondering – was I on track all along?

CHAPTER 23

The Ultimate Gift
Might be a Listening ear

Can I see a show of hands here? How many of you all look forward to really listening to someone who's very opinionated at the holiday table? How about "kind of" listening to that same person? Exactly as I anticipated, I didn't see a single hand go up. I wouldn't relish the idea either.

When we encounter brick walls of intolerance, extremism, or arrogance, I've learned that the best path forward might be to just talk or walk around the obstacle.

In many situations, with luck, engaged listening can turn differences of opinions into better understanding and therefore improved relationships.

Who among us doesn't enjoy telling their story? It has some universal appeal in the right environment. And we can provide that safe place and set the tone as we ask questions. Although true-false or specific questions may be relatively easy to come up with, they can actually be intimidating to the listener based on their current situation. They can also be very conducive to one-word answers, and they tend to funnel the conversation more than expand it.

The more specific the question, the less freedom the other conversant has to take the conversation where they're the most comfortable, and therefore the most honest.

Though I've clearly been guilty of doing the opposite, I do know better. The explicit questions that may have been delivered out of friendly curiosity may be received as a form of interrogation.

Questions can also be too broad. "What's up?" at least in my experience rarely goes anywhere useful unless "Not much" is what you're after. Asking expansive questions lets that long lost friend or relative take the driver's seat.

This type of question enables people to dig deeply and tell their story or just skim the surface - at their discretion. And that goes both ways. If there's some fairly balanced give and take and an expansive question is offered, there's lots of potential for a satisfying conversation.

Examples of expansive questions might be -
  What inspires you?
  Tell me about one of your heroes.
  What surprises you most about living in your new city?
  Does your work bring you satisfaction?
  What was the best part of your day so far?
  Can you help me understand how you came to that conclusion?
  Can you think of a downside to what you just suggested?
and the frequently useful prod - "Tell me more."

By truly listening, we provide a comfortable place for someone to speak - and be heard. One of the largest impediments to being a good listener is our continuous temptation to interject our views or insight. Truth be told, we typically spend considerably more effort trying to figure out how to respond than we do trying to understand or take in what another person is saying.

We know we're getting somewhere when either party thinks or admits - "I never thought of it that way."

I love the concept of the "Talking stick" initially used as a tool of indigenous democracies in our Pacific Northwest.   This would be passed around at council meetings, "Powwows" or when storytelling - to enable the speaker to have uncontested attention and the respect of those in attendance. That stick is part of their cultural world.

Expanding our perspective and understanding is what relationship building is all about - and to think, it can start merely by listening to someone's story.

CHAPTER 24

Savoring the Last Carefree Kiss

(Spoiler Alert - I Never Did)

A year and a half ago - I sat in our Lazy Boy chair, the spring sun yawning behind me. My pen crept thoughtfully across the notebook page as the boards of this century-old house came to life with the awakening of my bride above. Two minutes later, Emily awaits standing on the lowest stair in front of me. I arise as we trade our "Good Mornings," and walk over to the landing where we hug and kiss just like we've done a thousand times since moving here five years ago - and just as we thought we would do for many years to come.

Unbeknownst to both of us, that day would be different, ushering in a cascade of events, suffering and a roller-coaster of emotions. There would still be many more morning embraces at the base of those stairs, but today I stand there like a fool waiting for the boards to creak again.

CHAPTER 25

A Tiny Tribute to a Wonderful Soul

Emily - September 2024

The following is a slightly doctored version of the obituary honoring my editor, mentor, and beloved wife - Emily.

September 5, 1953 – March 3, 2025

Emily Lissandrello VanLaeys was born to Eugene and Mary Lissandrello in Nyack, New York and of late left the terra firma of Wisconsin for what she termed "The Great Adventure." Through it all, she was remarkably courageous, neither complaining nor thinking of her ten-month struggle with cancer as a battle - "dying is a normal part of life when you've lived as long as I have." And yet she would break down over the discovery of, yet another child lost to violence or abuse.

She spent most of her childhood in Sayville, NY, which is a small town on Long Island. It was there that she developed her love of the Great South Bay and eventually any and all bodies of water. Think - swimming, beautiful sunrises, spectacular sunsets, crashing waves and the peacefulness that we experience as we float on our backs in that which sustains us all.

Emily learned to read at a very early age and discovered the power of the written word. She loved exploring different cultures, historical periods, spiritual practices, and the different ways that people understand and experience God. She had a depth of compassion and empathy that transcended borders and the superficial differences that so many of us can't see beyond. Overflowing with love, neither bitterness nor hate ever found a place in her.

She was always a mother, wife and grand-mother extraordinaire, prioritizing family over everything. She was a mentor to her offspring and her husband who has been trying to grow up since they met in Yellowstone nearly five decades ago. Emily was a very humble person but most proud of the two children she and her husband, Mark, brought into this world.

Always curious, Emily never shied away from the deeper realities of other people's stories, be they while reading the pages of "The Diary of Anne Frank" or watching "War and Peace" as a ten-year-old. She was forever changed by those experiences as she divulged in her book "Dream Weaving - Using Dream Guidance to Create Life's Tapestry," which was published in January 2001, twenty-five years before this book you are currently reading.[3]

Over her years in Sayville, NY, Massachusetts, Alabama, Tennessee, Oneonta, NY and finally Wisconsin, she shared her work as a writer, and her unconditional kindness - all along the journey.

There were no "others" in her world. She had a most inclusive view of humanity and nature stressing the connections between all forms of life. Over the past five years, her newest passion was developing pollinator friendly "native gardens", and she reveled in the butterflies and birds which they attracted. She firmly believed that we are all interdependent in countless ways and connected via the loving and incomprehensible God who is within and beyond us.

A recent note to Emily in a get-well card expressed her gift so eloquently - "you have led a life of faithfulness, modeling what it means to live in Christ's light." Anyone who has been blessed with knowing her understands what he meant. I would be remiss if I didn't add that having Emily as my wife was a gift beyond measure.

---

[3]

Our marriage was not perfect, but we always made whatever compromises were necessary to ensure that it remained strong. A kiss - hug and an "I Love You" were accordingly the bookends of each day.

This past September Emily gave me specific instructions on what she did not want people to dwell on after she took leave from this life. In her own words,

"Please don't offer a chronological list of the schools I've attended or the jobs that I've held. That's not what my life was about. My life has been a lesson in love, and I hope that I learned how to do everything in love, whether it was office work, writing, mothering, cooking, gardening or performing weddings. Yes, it was easier to feel love in some moments than others, but love was always my goal."

In short, I believe Emily demonstrated with her life what a truly fine human being looks like. During her last few days, she made sure to tell us, "I am sorry to be leaving you, but don't weep for me.

I've had a good life, and I know it doesn't end when I leave this physical body . . . I look forward to exploring the multiverse beyond this earthly plane."

And it is both here and there where she'll continue to spread her light.

3) Dream Weaving – Using Dream Guidance to Create Life's Tapestry by Emily L VanLaeys © ARE Press 2001

CHAPTER 26

Grief and Gratitude in a Dead Heat

Disclaimer - There is very little that is unique to my loss or grief. This, and my recent posts are merely one person's take on an experience that is unfortunately a normal part of life. My hopes are that by sharing my perspective, I might help lighten the load of at least one person down the road.

If I had to describe the earliest days after Emily's departure, the words numb, and empty would certainly have come to mind. As you might imagine, those feelings are not conducive to writing, but sometimes even fleeting thoughts have an uncanny ability to sneak their way onto a blank page. Such was the case with "Savoring the Last Carefree Kiss" which I published a few days after what would have been our 48th anniversary.

I had just returned from a two-week venture down south only to rediscover a house stuffed with Emily's presence and yet strikingly empty. I had anticipated that my return and the looming "holiday" would be a challenge. But I was naive as to how much of a challenge it would be. Through the process, I've concluded that - so much of the grieving process is out of my control, but that's not to say that I can't nudge the helm of the ship.

I'm hoping that my recent wedding anniversary will be the lowest point on my path toward recovery. Healing has nothing to do with forgetting Emily, but everything to do with adapting to her loss. A dear friend Sharron, here on Substack put it so well – we will never recover from grief, we just learn how to make room for it.

My deep love for Emily is not lessened in any way as I share it with others. I see this as a major mid-course correction with rough waters still ahead, but I expect them to be of lesser magnitude and frequency – eventually.

I DO HAVE ALOT TO BE GRATEFUL FOR

Being immersed in the loving support of my family, my UCC church, neighbors, and friends far and wide including here, it's fair to say - my cup runneth over. I'll also add that my bride has been letting her presence be known.

I'm grateful that the people who mattered most to Emily had a year to express their gratitude for her presence in their lives and vice versa, and to say "goodbye." So many mourners would give anything to have had a five-minute conversation or reckoning with a loved one before they departed.

I'm grateful that Emily died at home as she wished, in the company of those she treasured. She was not deteriorating as a burden to others nor at the cost to others such as those fleeing continual violence in Gaza or Ukraine while deathly ill.

She and I were eternally grateful for a wonderful forty-eight years together along with our offspring whom we got to bond with and enjoy in countless ways. As one wise friend helped me realize - some of us who have once known love, might still be a tad bit jealous of your marriage which endured through so many years.

And I'm grateful that we had wonderful insurances to deal with most of the $700k worth of medical bills. The majority of people around the world would not have had access to the high level of care which provided several months of what Emily referred to as "icing." I would add that most Americans would not have had retirement funds to dig into for the substantial out-of-pocket expenses.

And then there was Hospice and their compassionate staff who helped enable Emily to lessen her symptoms and actually sleep. They were wonderful!

And last but certainly not least - I thank God every day for the opportunity to grow under such a remarkable, loving and kind mentor. Emily is in a better place, and I look forward to soaring with her again.

CHAPTER 27

"The Calm Beyond My Storms"

A song by Mark VanLaeys © September 2020

Sometimes, with a page turn there's a glimpse of things   that matter - A ray of light comes piercing through my walls.

As the moments turn to years, I see the gifts I took for granted, like your love for me, the calm between my storms.

I've always got my reasons, I'm so quick to bare my scars.

My days are filled with matter, yours with ether from the stars.

The waves of human failures keep me anchored to the past
as you follow streams of kindness to your sea,
as you follow streams of kindness to your peace

Sometimes this trip we-call-a-lifetime waves its banners,
    while others claim a tear from hazel eyes.

So many days I've wasted as I scale upon the worries
    of this place and time that you can see beyond.

My laws of human nature and of gravity and fire
    don't bind the realm of spirit to my spire.

But your patience and your gentle soul
    I thank God for each day

As you guide me through the calms between my storms
    As you love me to the calm beyond my storms

CHAPTER 28

Enlightened by Loss

I've always enjoyed taking on a good challenge and the surprises that go with it. The degree to which we truly live, sure seems to be influenced by how much we put ourselves "out there" to learn, and experience . . . and that unfortunately entails risk. With that in mind, I still can't remember signing up for the class where on *March 3rd,* 2025, I would lose my soulmate of 48 years to cancer. In so many ways it's all new, but in others, I find myself drawing from a deep well of prior losses and growth.

Significant loss has forced me to immerse myself in places, previously considered - too painful to even touch. But I'm not alone. I've been blessed with such a supportive family. A few people who were friends have now become dear friends. People who I hadn't even known two months ago have been key in 7helping me move forward. Songs that I'd never even heard of before have found their way on to my Pandora "shuffle mix." The most recent was Jimmy Buffet's - Breathe in, Breathe out, Move on." And they all contain healing salve.

Just for clarification, moving forward has nothing to do with letting go of the person we've lost. It has everything to do with - shining the right light on our memories and their place in our hearts.

So many times, over the years, I've found myself making judgements about the losses and grief of others. . . how it must have been so much worse, or so much easier for them than for others. And, I might have been right . . . or absolutely wrong. In hindsight I think I've probably been wrong more times than right. My assessments were always built upon my own experiences in life and tons of projections, not theirs.

There's absolutely no way I could have known or understood what inner strengths or weaknesses the grieving person carried into their loss. Nor could I have understood on any deep level the strengths of relationships between the departed and those left behind. Some would have been much better than I could have ever imagined, and some would have been the opposite. Were there substantial unresolved conflicts? What were the most recent conversations between the departed and those left behind? We're talking multivariable calculus, and who among us are adept at that!

Grief is as unique as the person suffering from it and the relationship that they had with the departed. If my eyes are open, I will encounter people who are in all stages of grief in the months and years to come. Anything I've learned in the last six or so months might come to the surface and be helpful.

Love is all about cutting people slack. It's letting them grow in the direction and at the pace that they are most comfortable with. The people who have stood out as the most helpful to me have done just that. The kind pat on my shoulder as I raced to the exit door after the Easter Service, the gentle squeeze of my forearm as another walked by, the texts with the praying hands, or the patience waiting for the right time to call me. And then there's the newsy updates from a loved one to remind me that there is still so much to smile about. Every one of them was a nudge in the right direction.

I need to be OK with the fact that when someone else is grieving, my timing for what should be most helpful may not always match theirs. The recent invitations for meals, prods to get back into the groove etc. have all been so well-timed and therefore especially helpful. And I'm so grateful for all of the above.

One of the more touching kindnesses was from a friend who handed me a beautiful poem, and some homemade muffins on May 3rd - while gently reminding me that today especially, you might need these.

CHAPTER 29

A Eulogy for my Bride

I've hesitated for months to even try to honor Emily because she was so complex and spiritually attuned. But here is my feeble attempt -

Photo by Author – Mark VL

We first met while working in Yellowstone National Park, in late summer 1977. After a few light conversations over meals in the staff cafeteria, I invited Emily for a date to a ghost town north of Yellowstone. It was there, late in the afternoon, that we wondered into an abandoned cemetery - and talked about everything from baby's memorialized with tiny remnants of tombstones, to life after death, and reincarnation. From that moment, I realized that Emily Jean Lissandrello had one foot on this planet and the other - not in the clouds but in the heavens - and those were limitless.   She was and I'm sure still is, an explorer of the light.

Emily has devoured thousands of books, sifting through the lives and challenges of people around the globe and throughout time. She was especially intrigued by widely divergent spiritual leaders of substance. And she was most saddened by the agenda driven, and exclusive nature of so many religions which have been used as tools to separate people into the worthy and the unworthy. Jesus never did that, and either did Emily.

But before I go on, and lift her onto some pedestal, let me acknowledge - she did have her flaws. For starters, even though she very rarely got angry, she did have one four-letter word that she dropped way too often. This included a month before she died when someone I know accidently punched out a glass globe on one of our lamps while demonstrating a karate block. I can't say the word here because we're in a church - BUT I can say, it began with an M and ended with ARK. And it was always delivered with a lot of passion.

From my perspective, she had other "flaws." She never seemed to be able to emulate the most natural of human tendencies. For instance, even though she had a strong sense of right and wrong, she never learned how to be judgmental of the people who held different views.

Even though she was generally soft-spoken, she never learned how to bite her tongue when her inner voice told her to speak up against injustice or on behalf of the disadvantaged.

She never learned how to triangulate against anyone regardless of how "wrong" they appeared to be.   And she never learned how to carry heavy burdens such as fear, malice, regrets, bitterness, or hatred.

Some might say that Emily marched to a different drummer, but I would say she merely listened to and followed her higher angels. And that served her, and those who knew her - very well.

We were lifelong partners on our quest to bring a little more light into this often too dark world - and Emily did just that with her blog - Building Bridges of Oneness, and more recently with her passion for pollinator friendly - native gardening. She was always trying to bridge those gaps between earth and heaven, between peoples of all faiths and cultures, and between human beings and nature.

Emily never played the "Poor Me" card. She went to the gym with a decreasing frequency starting around December. Sometime in January, I saw a new woman there, a little younger than us, and introduced myself. Then I called over and introduced "Robin" to Emily, who was sporting her bright-colored chemo cap. They talked for a few minutes that day and then maybe five to ten minutes, a couple weeks later.

Though Emily stopped going to the gym shortly thereafter, I didn't see Robin myself until six weeks after Emily passed. We exchanged pleasantries and then with all the innocence in the world, Robin asked - "so how's Emily doing?" When I said she died March 3rd, this mere acquaintance started sobbing. After a long, consoling hug she was able to get out the words - "I just really liked her." And that was the effect that Emily could have. She connected, and that person knew they were loved.

She was a blessing to all those who stepped within her ever-enlarging circle. To quote the words of Joy Fuller, from her book entitled, *The Glorious Presence,*[4] "Living love into expression is the greatest and most exciting adventure anyone can experience." That is exactly what Emily spent her life doing here - and will do - as she ventures into those limitless heavens beyond.

4)DeVorss & Company© 1981 Joy Fuller

_____

[4]

CHAPTER 30

What's that Person Juggling?

When it comes to juggling, I've never been able to break even the one-minute mark with three tennis balls. Anyone seeing what I was juggling could have made the call - "Hey, that guy is a crappy juggler." And they would have been correct. All three variables were right out there in plain sight.

But what about when they're not?

Photography by Alessio Soggetti © Unsplash

Twelve years ago, as an adaptive ski instructor in upstate New York, one of my first days of our annual training was alongside Don. He was a spirited guy I'd just met and talked to earlier that morning. I'd taken note of his Army cap which covered some short grey hair. Over the course of the day, as we traversed some of the steepest runs on the mountain, I conceded the fact that he was a better skier than me.

At the end of the day, we resumed talking and made our way down to the locker room. While I effortlessly took off one of my ski boots, I couldn't help but notice Don slowly removing each ski boot along with a custom made, below the knee, leg prosthesis.

Don had left both of his legs in Vietnam. I trained and or volunteered with him for seven years and never once heard him mention his disability to anyone.

Going even further back, when we lived in a moderately large southern city, I was a volunteer at a telephone crisis center. We'd had maybe twenty hours of training on effective listening; then turned loose with our list of community resources and well-wishes. We were the suicide hotline of the day, and every caller remained anonymous, as did the volunteers. I heard all too many heart-wrenching stories and didn't always "let them go," as was certainly advisable. It was difficult to keep my imagination in check.

Seeing a teen on a bus with a disheveled mother, I'd go through my mental files. Could he be the thirteen-year-old boy whose father left home, because his mother would never stop drinking? That would be the same mother who frequently left him for hours on end while she went out for a pack of cigarettes.

Waiting in line at the local convenience store, I would notice things like the completely uninvested cashier. A dazed look and no eye contact with anyone. And I would wonder, is she the woman in her "mid-twenties" who had called a few months ago? She would be the one who divulged that she hated her father but knew that was "wrong." He had "loved her so much" that he slept with her whenever her mother was out of town - but she didn't like to talk about that.

Why such long faces on such a beautiful day?

We've all been there, unfortunately some of us on the wrong side of the observation. Everyone's enjoying themselves, families chatting around the picnic tables, like at our local ice-cream place. All too often there are "those people" who just can't be happy.

There were two at the nearby table - a sixtyish-year old woman, sitting speechless across from a middle-aged woman who had a gold ring on her hand. It's not like they were distraught, but they were just so friggin' somber. I was watching four kids pick through flavors at the window, when my ears perked up as the two women broke their silence.

I took a fleeting glance and caught the younger woman wiping her eyes as she slid an envelope across the table. Two minutes later it still sat un-opened next to a full bowl of melting ice cream. As the younger woman became more animated, I was able to hear her words, and then the crying. "I'm so sorry Mom," followed by something about insurance, and then an emotionally laden, "They say Austin and I are just too old to try again!" Though the mom tried to comfort her, no one near them could escape their suffering.

Life on this planet is certainly a challenge for everyone - but to widely varying degrees. So many times, I've fallen into the trap where I find myself judging someone else for being in a funk or being so downright nasty.

And I ask myself - could it really be all that bad? Well, sometimes the answer is - yes.

CHAPTER 31

A Vet – Stranded, Broke & Hungry

A couple years ago, I got a call from my wife ten minutes after she left to go grocery shopping. She had a strained, intensity to her voice. "There's a guy on the corner with a backpack and a cardboard sign - 'Vet - stranded, broke, and hungry.' "It's a crime!" We'd seen variations on the theme play out so often, that we almost had a protocol.

Photo by Mark VanLaeys

I grabbed a few protein bars, my motorcycle jacket, and headed off. Even though I've probably reached out to more strangers than the average bloke, it's always a little unsettling. We're not used to talking to those outside our typical circles.

When eye to eye with someone who lives on the fringes, it's easy to default to - we probably don't have anything in common. But as the years roll by, I'm finding more times than not - we do. I just have to dig deeper sometimes than others.

Ten minutes later I pulled up and parked in a nearby lot. There he was, a guy "pushin' eighty," with a worn-out hat, the requisite backpack, and dark shades. I introduced myself and asked - "So how are you doing today?" With a toothless grin and a heavy Tennessee drawl, "Miguel" responded, "doin' pretty well."

"Where are you headed?" He responded saying something about his sister, Nashville, some arranged ride, Washington, Dakota, and Nashville. My BS meter flickered. He definitely had a southern accent; but between that, his lack of teeth and occasional traffic, I was confused at best.

I tried to get him to clarify. "Can you tell me again where you said your sister lived . . . and where you're headed?" He looked at me, his face tightening, and went silent. I grabbed for a lifeline - it was not a long stretch.

"When I graduated from college back in the late seventies, I hitchhiked a lot - close to fifteen thousand miles. I've got a bit of a soft spot for people on the road."

Sensing I wasn't going to run off, he slowly explained how he'd gone from his home in Nashville to visit his younger sister in Washington state. The trip was going fine until the ride that she'd arranged for his return trip fell through. He'd managed to get a ride to one of the Dakotas but then had to collect a number of rides to work his way to Wisconsin. At this point, he was headed south toward Nashville where his 17-year-old dog awaited his return.

And he opened up. "Back in 1972, I had just gotten back from Nam. I didn't get the welcome I was expecting, and my head was really f'cked up . . . I ended up on the road for seven years goin' nowhere . . . till I finally stopped drinkin'."

From an otherwise empty front pocket, Miguel pulled out his AA medallion commemorating his first year of sobriety forty plus years ago. He held it for me to read. "This is my reminder to never go back. I don't need the drink; I got rid of my demons."

We shared our experiences riding the rails and though mine was short and hair raising, his was a protracted ordeal. He learned how to work the system in the process. There were actually maps that included all the main freight routes across the U.S. And they were available to anyone for a fee. Who would have imagined?

Miguel also pointed out: "Even hobos can be generous." One had given him the prized government map when they had crossed paths on a freight car. Gone were some of the unknowns and risks of rail travel.

I talked with him for roughly a half hour and though not one tooth ever made an appearance, he certainly laughed and smiled. I felt we had made some connections, but the truth was hidden behind those dark glasses.

We both shared memories of those years when we each traveled to find ourselves - me after sixteen years of trudging through books, and him after two years of trudging through hell. All of those experiences shaped us, and for better or worse, our futures. There were opportunity costs we each paid for the choices we made back then. Unfortunately, he keeps paying for his.

One of the highlights of my short time with Miguel was seeing a woman in her mid-thirties walk over from the lot next to my motorcycle. She offered a bright smile and heartfelt words of encouragement. She then placed some folded bills in his hands and returned to one of the most dilapidated cars I've ever seen.

We were both touched by her kindness and generosity. We shook hands and he thanked me twice for my travel money. "I'm going to remember this as coming from my brother who's gone on - his name was Mark, too."

A Mid-book Invitation

I really appreciate each one of you spending your time and energy here as I share my experiences and subsequent reflections.

Your thoughts are also valued, so please consider leaving a review of this book on Amazon or via your e-reader @ Amazon.com: Morphing into a Better World: Musings on Encounters, Connections, and Hope eBook : VanLaeys, Mark: Kindle Store

Thank you

CHAPTER 32

Listening, Respect, and Self Discovery

I'm gonna step out on a limb here and suggest that most people are not great listeners. Sure, we all have our moments, but is the average conversation we participate in an actual exchange of ideas? Or is it more like a food fight, in which each participant spends most of their time strategizing how to get the next "shot" to stick?

Listening is the cornerstone of effective communication.

In another chapter exploring this topic, I acknowledged that at times I've demonstrated really crappy listening skills, while at others, I've apparently risen to the occasion and provided a safe place for people to speak. As a physician assistant who frequently ran late, my patients would periodically placate me by declaring some version of - "I don't mind waiting for you, because you always take the time to listen to me."

As I recently pondered those fine memories, I started to pat myself on the back. But it didn't take long for me to acknowledge that those reassurances were made years ago. I started questioning - have I been losing whatever listening skills I once had, at a time when using those skills is more important than ever?

Jeanne Malmgren, who writes "Rx Nature" on Substack, left me a very elucidating comment regarding a former newsletter of mine. As a psychotherapist, she introduced me to the term "Unconditional Positive Regard," and over the next couple days, I had an "aha" moment.

Though I learned that the professional term is quite nuanced, I'm particularly drawn to the simplicity and power of those three words as they're strung together. They capture what I tried to practice throughout my career in medicine and as a volunteer community mediator. Most importantly, unconditional positive regard may be what's been missing in some of my more heated verbal exchanges. And that has led me to reflect upon my recent encounters - some that have worked, and some that haven't.

In my last chapter here about a stranded Veteran, I recounted a positive interaction with a guy stuck in my hometown. Though I'm sure we would have disagreed on a lot of issues, he had my unconditional positive regard.

So why, I ask, didn't a long-lost friend get the same respect when she suggested something I thought was almost farcical? I really think it was because she made one "wrong" comment that temporarily turned her into an adversary - not worthy of my "positive regard."

On reflection, I realize that if someone doesn't challenge my way of thinking, I'm respectful of them and try to use my best listening skills. But the inverse is unfortunately all too true.

It is never a conscious choice; it's a default behavior that can slip out if I'm not paying attention. Those with different views can unknowingly become my second-class citizens. And that is something that needs my serious attention. It's immature, arrogant, and it kills communication where it's most needed.

Aiming to internalize "Unconditional Positive Regard," should be much like archery for us novices. We shouldn't beat ourselves up because we don't hit the bullseye each time, as long as we're getting closer to that center.

CHAPTER 33

The Opposite of Being Poor
Is Having Enough

It's fair to say that there are countless ideas of what the words "poor" and "enough" mean. I'm reminded of the late Supreme Court Justice Potter Steward when trying to define "pornography". He famously said something like - "I'll know it when I see it".

Images and hot button topics quickly come to mind when we think of "poverty" - maybe news coverage from Africa or the slums in our nearest city, food stamps, the homeless guy with the cup or the child depending on school lunches for her daily nutrition.

How about the word "enough"? That's a tough one because so few of us ponder what that actually is. Wealth and "enough" are rarely considered synonyms. I've met and worked with lots of people who, by all appearances, were dirt poor. Whether it was in Ethiopia, or across the US, sprinkled among these common folk were those who had enough. Just enough food, shelter, faith, companionship, love, peace of mind, and sense of purpose. They were an inspiring lot.

On most days I really feel I have enough. The older I get, however, the more I "lose sleep" over two groups - those who truly don't have enough, and those who will *never* **think** they have enough.

CHAPTER 34

A Stolen God and a Corn Moon

Photography by Mark VanLaeys

Recently, a friend of mine and I decided to meet along Lake Geneva's shore her in Wisconsin to take in a sunset and the forecasted full moon - officially dubbed a "Corn Moon." As we settled down on our park bench, we took in the classy snacks she'd made and the simplest of life's pleasures.

To our left was a roughly ten-year-old boy - alone, playing in the sand, and muttering to himself, or maybe to a character in his sandscape. In front of us was a sedge-lined concrete path and beyond that, moored boats on a glassy lake beneath a few waning clouds. To our right the brightest of orbs was settling down.

Over the next hour we watched the parade of humanity stroll by - some with dogs, some alone and in contemplation, and others immersed in bright-hearted conversations. As the sun had clearly turned in for the night, a young man was slowly peddling by us on his high-wheeled "penny farthing."

As we said hello, "Austin" stepped down and returned the greeting. Over the next 15 or so minutes, this cyclist and daytime forklift operator shared his passion as a small crowd gathered. A middle-aged woman, "Barbara" joined in with our conversation.

Diverse groups of people continued to meander on by. This included eight or so snowbirds who had met each other in Florida years ago but were at the lake as part of one of their summer reunions. As the phones flashed away, a young woman wearing a hijab apologetically squeezed in to capture the visual. And that sandcastle architect had stopped his construction and was all ears.

It became quite clear that Austin was a regular there in Lake Geneva, but also anywhere where he could, in his own words, "bring a smile to people's faces." Barbara quickly added - "and that you certainly do." To our surprise, he responded - "with one exception."

He then recounted a recent experience where he was riding his bike through one of the large regional music festivals, when one party reveler called him the "N-word," as he rode by. Though Austin went on to say that the event was notorious for being rowdy and drug-ridden, there was no apparent reason for the bizarre and racist comment. That said, Barbara's follow-up comment was almost equally deranged. "That's what happens when you take God out of the classroom."

Try as I may, I can't wrap my head around the concept that - we're going to blame drug abuse, one of our nation's worst societal problems, on "those people" who miraculously extracted the "creator of all that is" from the buildings where our children are educated.

Let me start by saying that God, Shaddai, Yahweh, Allah, Adoni, Elohim or my favorite label - Divine Mystery, cannot be defined, extracted or changed to meet human needs or political agendas – though countless people have tried.

To remove God from the classroom would be akin to extracting love and divine mystery - from our random encounters on the lake, the everyday miracle of the setting sun or that huge, beautiful moon which lit each of our ways home.

CHAPTER 35

Help From Beyond in Troubled Waters

Photo by Mark VanLaeys

"You must do the thing you think you cannot do"

Eleanor Roosevelt

The above quote has inspired and motivated me for most of my life. It was lovingly needlepointed for me by my wife Emily during the 1980's. Though the framed artwork did not survive our move to Wisconsin five years ago, its message has been especially poignant to me since Emily's March 3rd "passing."

Within ten days of her taking leave of her cancer-ridden body, I was on-line searching for a cruise to take me away from this home and the ever-present reminders of her absence. We both loved the ocean, the openness, the beaches and the escape from responsibilities. As a bonus, I could liberate some of her ashes in the types of places that always brought her joy. I looked forward to the opportunity to reminisce and spend the week on my oceanside balcony with my guitar and endlessly swirling thoughts.

So, on March nineteenth, with an almost perverse sense of relief, we headed due south to the port city of New Orleans. Emily's straw hat rode shotgun, and both of our wedding rings clinked together on a braided chain around my neck. Twelve hours later, I walked into a Mexican Restaurant in Hernando, Mississippi. As I approached the "Hostess" sign, I encountered a man in his mid-eighties getting ready to leave, as his son went to retrieve their car. When our eyes met, he sent me a huge laugh-grin, "Did you just lose somebody?"

Half confused and half perturbed, I asked him - why would you say that? He responded with an indignant - "You've got it right there on your chest," at which point I looked down and got my first good laugh in months. I explained that the t-shirt I was wearing actually had the letters RPI, which was short for

Rensselaer Polytechnic Institute which my son attended in New York. I mentioned that I'd had that shirt for fifteen years and was pleased that someone had finally noticed it - giving me an opportunity to talk about one of my kids.

And then I shared that I did lose my wife a couple weeks earlier. After a very sincere apology, he responded, "I lost my wife many years ago and I'm never getting over it." Though those words left me with sadness, they were also a nuanced challenge.

Fast forward to Sunday, March 23rd. I'm on the 15th deck of the enormous Norwegian Cruise Line - "Getaway." It's late afternoon and I'm one of hundreds of spectators watching the shoreline of the Mississippi edge by. We were only two hours into our seven-day trip when two teenagers approached a sixtyish year-old guy leaning on the nearby railing. "Mom's pretty sloshed, so we escorted her back to the room for a nap." After a few words back and forth, the two guys headed off to explore.

I made a comment to tone down the awkwardness and within ten minutes, a conversation about parked barges along the shoreline had turned into the sharing of our personal flying stories. He'd been an aviator for seven years and me, for half a century. We each found some solace there in our happy place.

Since this wasn't my first cruise, I'd been braced for the possibility that the trip might worsen the foreign sense of loneliness which I now carried. There would be close to thirty-five-hundred guests packed into the 1100-foot-long ship, and probably 99.9% of them would be in groups of friends, as couples, or in families. Here, within two hours, I was talking one on one with a stranger. Before we parted, we introduced ourselves, both of us "Marks." Our encounter eased my mind a bit, and the name-match got filed away as a welcome coincidence.

The first morning on the ship, I randomly threw on my recently sink-washed "RPI" shirt. As I entered the already crowded Garden Cafe Restaurant, a gentle rain clung to the large glass windows alongside endless rows of tables. This sprawling buffet, on both sides of the ship, would feed thousands of guests over the next few hours.

I can't remember what I had to eat that morning, because those thoughts were dwarfed by what happened as I weaved my way through the tables to leave. A middle-aged couple were seated almost in my path when the pig-tailed guy in front of me inquired - "Are you a Rensselaer guy . . . I'm from New Jersey?"

I responded - I'm not, but my son went there. He looked curious so I continued - it's ironic that you should ask. I explained that no one in fifteen years had ever commented on this shirt - until four days ago. I had just started to tell them about the elderly guy in Mississippi, when he abruptly stood up and gave me a seriously long bear hug. Somehow, he managed to get out the words - "I noticed you were wearing the two rings around your neck. That's the same thing that I did when my wife died."

We commiserated for close to an hour that first day, with his partner leaving to give us some space. Though he was obviously still hurting from the tragic loss of his wife five years earlier, he dug deeply to learn about my situation, as he shared his. He also touched on some of the coping mechanisms which he'd found helpful. Before parting that day, he inquired, "I hope you don't mind, but I'd like to check in with you each day." In retrospect, I think he was worried. He alone would know how tempting those low railings might be for a person who'd lost so much.

Even though he was there with his two teenage kids and lady friend, he did find time each day to find me and talk about Emily and my future, while he reminisced about his late wife and his. I will always remember him as an exceptionally empathetic guy, and his name was also - "Marc".

Sunrises can certainly be awe-inspiring but, throw in a seriously elevated vantage point, a panoramic view, and add a looming storm, and you've got a memorable gem. I had that and more the third morning of the cruise as I brushed elbows with a beautiful soul, who happened to be pretty as well.

With blue eyes and blond hair, the fiftyish year-old woman had taken a vacant spot maybe twenty feet away from me, along the top deck railing. I made some initial comment which organically drifted toward a conversation about the sunrises at sea, the varied impacts of cruise ships, the little evidence of nature we'd seen out at sea. . . and the dolphins I wish she'd seen the day before. We talked about our children, including her teenagers who were onboard along with her husband. . . and that led to one more variant of the question - "are you here with family?"

As I started to explain my situation, she was deeply saddened. Being speechless, her glistening eyes turned toward the long-completed sunrise. I'd known this big-hearted woman for a mere half hour, and yet her response was not surprising. It wasn't so much the words she'd spoken as the kindness and love she emanated then and over the next half hour.

Eventually my growling stomach told me it was time to depart so, hoping I would see her again, I introduced myself. She responded with a most gracious smile and an extended hand, "I'm Emily." Returning her smile and fighting back tears, I shared - and that was also my wife's name.

So, the question I was left with is –

Which is the greater folly - to believe that out of the 5000 people on the ship, I just randomly ran into those three valuable encounters, or that just maybe, they might have been - divinely orchestrated?

CHAPTER 36

A Rescue Mission
For Our Highest Self

"Growing with the Mirror" photograph - Mark VanLaeys

The ultimate Us AND Them challenge may be to learn how to live in meaningful relationship with our highest self. That would be the one that always errs on the side of moral integrity and courage. Whatever our aspirations, our highest self could be the one we wanted to be when we grew up. How do we set with that person today?

Who were our heroes? Who have they become? If we're struggling to come up with ideas, maybe more importantly, we should be asking - who were our heroes before they were cast aside . . . maybe by an ever-growing reverence for material things, cynicism, or a contracting world view?

Have idols replaced our heroes?

Author Peter Gibbon, who wrote *A Call to Heroism* says "Idol means uncritical worship. . . unthinking admiration."

In the same decade, American psychologist Frank Farley, surveyed people across the US about their heroes. He concluded, "all heroes share certain traits – courage and strength, generosity, honesty, expertise, a tendency toward risk-taking."

I would also add that heroes are notorious for giving sacrificially - denying themselves as they prioritize another.

Who do we most admire today, and why? Could it have previously been someone for whom our modern-day world makes little room?

Maybe there's a conflict between our dreams and this person we've become, with our vision being dulled to the point where we can't even perceive the qualities that we once revered. Maybe we've become so cynical that we've lost sight of a realistic and tangible role model who could rescue this embattled world from itself.

On a personal level, the question which keeps coming around is

 - - *Have I given up on being my highest self, and when is it prudent to give up on that quest?*

CHAPTER 37

Desensitization –
Maybe a Viable Option

I'm not a - walk slowly into a cold ocean - type guy. Unlike Emily who would do just that over the course of five minutes, my modus operandi would be to dive in as quickly as possible.

That's not because I'm courageous or have a high "pain" threshold; that would be Emily. I've merely done the math and for me, it only makes sense to transition through the misery as quickly as possible - all done, now I can enjoy myself.

I fully recognize that grief will never be over and done with. But, at least for me, timely and deliberate actions seem to help me usher what was initially an agonizing pain, toward the background where it's now more of a dull ache.

The preceding year's photo taken by a waitress at Madrez Cafe

Yesterday, after working for several days on a neglected lawn and Emily's overgrown gardens, I figured it was time for a break and headed out for a motorcycle ride - destination unknown.

I was maybe ten miles out of town, headed north when I passed the "Madrez Cafe." Since it was there that we'd shared our last enjoyable coffee date together, I felt compelled to make a U-turn.

Five minutes later I was seated at the same table we'd been to six months earlier and yes, it was sad. I reflected on all that Emily had been through over the interim. Between sips of good strong coffee and bites of a cinnamon bun, I was able to appreciate that her suffering was indeed over, and that mine was beginning to fade.

I located the above picture on my phone and was quite sure it was taken by the woman who seated me. But when I asked her if she remembered taking it, she was non-committal. As I told her that my wife had died in early March, she was not hesitant in offering her sincere sympathy.

I still wonder what prompted me to tell a stranger about my loss. It sure didn't make her day any brighter, but maybe I sensed that she was the kind of person who wouldn't mind taking on a tiny bit of my load - because I did walk out feeling a little lighter.

From the cafe, I headed north and within five minutes felt a characteristic ping on my neck which was followed by a progressive stinging sensation . . . and within minutes a palpable welt. The wind in my face is an important part of why I like to ride on two wheels.

I'm periodically reminded that there's a small price to pay for that indulgence but also a larger benefit. All that was present when I got home was a small red dot, when – years ago I would have had a sore spot for days.

Maybe along the same lines – I'll eventually become immune, and it won't be the least bit painful to have a cup of coffee at one of our old haunts.

CHAPTER 38

Insights on "Never-enough-itis"

NEI from Diagnosis to Treatment

Many of you reading this article may not be aware of a recently identified, but long existing illness called neverenoughitis. "NEI" is a spectrum disorder which has mushroomed to epidemic proportions during this and the last century.

Photography by Karolina Grabowska © - Unsplash

Though there are pockets documented worldwide, it is particularly prevalent in the United States. Over the next few minutes, I'd like to share the preliminary findings regarding this newly elucidated and potentially fatal disorder - *which I just made up.*

What it is -

Derived from the Latin - numquam satis itis, neverenoughitis is characterized by insatiable and maladaptive consumption or acquisition. Though this malady certainly has features in common with addictions or obsessions, the origins, development and manifestations of NEI are much more complex.

Typically, this characteristic pursuit is completely detached from any concern regarding its consequences for others - beyond relatively small familial or social circles. It frequently involves sensory gratification with various levels of immorality and criminality.

As with any spectrum disorder, the traits may be fairly common across populations but in effected individuals, they are pervasive. The human tendencies toward compassion and or reason have also been suppressed if not totally lost. Those affected are much more concerned about their own heightened level of comfort today than they are about the health of the planet which will sustain their own progeny down the road.

While all types of substance abuse are complex, a large portion of those with addictions may have foundational levels of NEI.

Typical victims of neverenoughitis -

The rising entertainer, successful business leader, or esteemed preacher who turn to illicit drugs or extra-marital affairs to fill the emptiness which the disorder creates.

The premium athlete who is at the top of his or her game and yet still feels compelled to cheat.

Any middle or upper-class individual who makes critical personal or family choices based solely on ever-increasing monetary acquisition.

The millionaire and billionaire elites who joust for huge tax cuts which will undermine the programs that large portions of Americans have contributed to and rely on for their very survival.

The politicians or entrepreneurs whose ceaseless quest for more power and wealth comes at the clear expense of the freedoms, health and welfare of the masses for generations to come.

Treatment options -

Cognitive Behavioral Therapy can certainly be helpful but there are no certified counselors in this new and burgeoning field.

Reality testing in conjunction with a slow reintroduction to everyday people who exhibit no signs or symptoms of this disorder.

Keeping a gratitude journal to gain a healthier perspective.

Literally giving away money in sacrificial amounts to causes that are not self-serving, can remove the false sense of powerlessness which can accompany advanced NEI.

Reasons for hope -

While NEI is a chronic disorder it has many variants suggesting that there are both recessive and dominant genes which produce different phenotypes. So, stay tuned as the research results start to pour in.

Many of those who suffer from this disorder will eventually go into remission as they mature, though childlike patterns tend to persist if reinforced through adulthood.

CHAPTER 39

Growing Beyond Assumptions to Respect

Photo by Mark VanLaeys

I had walked past the army-green behemoth several times. But it was out of the way, distanced by a half-a-dozen campsites and maybe an assumption or two. As I neared the end of my several day camping trip, the smoke drifting from their fire-pit drew me closer.

The first thing I realized was that the flag hanging off the rear of the truck was not in adoration of anyone. Nor was it there to denigrate anyone else. It was there to bring attention to Tim's proud service in the U.S. Navy as a Seabee - derived from the initials for "Construction Battalion." I would soon learn that it was this work to create local bases of operations that took this intelligent man around the world where he worked with fellow service members but also locals - giving him a very wide frame of reference.

After an initial matched pair of greetings, I started off asking if they were the builders of this impressive home on wheels. Tim took that ball and ran with it, while Julie worked on dinner at the fire pit, periodically chiming in with poignant contributions.

As it turned out, Tim built this RV over the course of years. He designed it around a large 1966 Jeep Kaiser frame, the container from a large box truck and the diesel engine from an old school bus. Inside and out, it emanated a level of ingenuity I suspect few of us have. After leaving the Navy, he went into law enforcement eventually becoming the police chief of their northern Wisconsin city.

I noticed the very well-made, personalized fire pit "ring" and discovered that it was the creation of their nephew, a metal worker. I mentioned that I had taken advantage of a local metalsmith when I needed a counterweight fabricated for the ultralight airplane which I'd built. Tim expressed a surprising level of understanding. He explained that it was his responsibility to make certain that the weights and balances of the military aircraft were maintained as they loaded cargo - "otherwise airplanes will stop flying regardless of how large they are."

Julie brought up the extreme poverty so prevalent in many of the countries where Tim worked and passed on the story of one man who served the last chicken he owned to Tim and his fellow Seabees - refusing any payment for his generosity. Tim added that the man would eventually find their gift, which one of them had hidden in his mud hut.

As he wove stories from his past and toward the present, I let him know I appreciated the wide perspective he gained through so much travel and exposure to different mindsets. I juxtaposed that with the volunteer work I'd done with medical mission work abroad and teaching adaptive sports to disabled veterans here in the US. He expressed his astonishment that so many people were content to never even step outside the county they grew up in. All three of us shared a mutual respect for so many blessings that were foundational to this country and yet rare in others.

I was pleasantly surprised that he was so easy to talk to, but with friends coming over for dinner, things got cut short. I suspect that otherwise we could have dipped further beneath the surface on some controversial subjects with an actual exchange of ideas. One of his main hobbies was "making old things run longer." In fact, he usually drove an Oldsmobile from the 1980's which had 300 plus thousand miles on it. He mentioned that rejuvenating well-used things leaves a smaller environmental footprint than buying new.

We never talked politics per se, but there was one solitary point of departure when one of us brought up the discord that plagued our nation. Tim threw in the old cliche - "Love it or Leave it," which I challenged. Would you agree that the foundation of this country - the Constitution, was centered around the protection of the interests of wealthy, white, male, landowners? He did agree and hopefully had some lingering thoughts about my follow up question - doesn't it seem equally important that we ensure that the rights and privileges of this country are extended to all Americans? And I did see a pensive nod.

One of his final comments which left me thinking was - "We need to get a better hold on what it means to be an American." As we had exchanged ideas for half an hour, I had a strong sense that we'd walk on some common ground there.

CHAPTER 40

Evolution -
Good Conversations
Around Large Tables

Photography by Mathieu Oden, Unsplash

When we think of the words "peace, or peace-making," we might default to thoughts of the big conflicts - "out there." Things like the unfathomable horror in Ukraine, or the worst neighborhoods of Chicago, might come to mind.

But what about the conflicts residing closer to home? Consider the countless military personnel who are trained or conditioned to dehumanize the generic "other" as a pretext for killing in wars. What happens when that "other," a few years later, moves into the house next door?

What about the indigenous American farmer forced to till dry, sandy soil because they can't afford the land with the dark rich soil taken from their great grandparents. Or consider the uneducated and ill- informed elderly woman, struggling to make ends meet, not knowing that there's real assistance available at that "dreaded government office" a few blocks away.

There can be no enduring tranquility here in our homeland when we accept the exploitation or neglect of our most vulnerable as a cost of retaining the status quo.

CHAPTER 41

Regina – Surely One in a Billion!

How do I, as a garden-variety Joe, write with any clarity about a young woman who seemed so angelic? I met Regina when she was in her late twenties. She was a completely blind quadriplegic with no motor function below her neck. And yet she seemed clearly grateful to be alive. I could never have hoped to cross paths with such an extraordinary human being and yet I did!

Forty years ago, my wife signed up for a weekend spirituality conference an hour north of New York City. I just tagged along and figured there might be something to learn. I had all-but zoned out as the main speaker started her required announcements such as the direction to the fire exits and restrooms, but she also passed on a request for someone to help an attendee who had special needs.

After the morning presentations, I headed toward the podium where Regina and her wheelchair were being pushed by her sixtyish-year-old mother. She explained that she mainly needed someone to transfer her daughter back and forth

163

between the wheelchair and the bed. Pity crept in when I saw Regina ensnared by straps from head to toe, but nothing could constrain her appreciative smile.

Over the next couple of days, we got a tiny glimpse of who Regina had been, and who she had blossomed into. Her dream as a senior in high school had been to become a concert pianist, but a rare, non-cancerous tumor had wrapped itself around the base of her brain. She and her mom were cautioned that the lengthy, involved procedure to excise the lesion would affect at least her breathing, vision and motor function but to unknown degrees. Either way, it could also prolong her life. It did all the above.

Regina's vision was completely gone, and being unable to use her hands, learning to read Braille was not an option. Her devoted mother apparently fed her a steady diet of audio books, and Regina attended college. Over the next eight years she earned her bachelor's degree in one of the social sciences.

Although she spoke relatively few words, and softly due to her impaired pulmonary function, everybody listened when Regina spoke. She was able to "write" by blowing short or long puffs into a small tube which triggered a transducer which in turn fed into a primitive computer.

I'm truly at a loss for words as I try to convey what it was like to be around Regina. She was a highly spiritual person as was her mother. They had a homecare attendant in NYC and came to the conference with the attitude that "God will provide, as He always has." I don't remember Regina ever talking about herself.

We spent hours together, and both she and her mother exuded gratitude for my help with issues like her neurogenic bowel and bladder dysfunction. I don't remember her ever being apologetic for the indignities because they were just a fact of life.

And, she never once pulled out the victim card. I don't even think she owned one.   Regina garnered respect for just being her authentic self. She returned to each presentation and breakout session with kindness, humility and insight beyond her years.

The most telling experience I had was when I sat across from Regina at a long dinner table - and we were all talking about the human tendency to judge. I shared an involved story about an acquaintance named "Brad Anderson." He was a fiftyish-year-old guy who had been the head of the recreation department at our large Methodist Church in Eastern Tennessee.

Brad always seemed down. I would try to engage him, but he seemed to strain to even look me in the eye or say hello.

At that time, I was working for four orthopedic surgeons as their physician assistant. One morning I got a page from the ER to come see a 79-year-old woman, who'd broken her hip while walking across the kitchen. X-rays confirmed that Emma Anderson had what's called a pathological fracture where a bone breaks, in this case because it was replaced by a tumor from her metastatic breast cancer. At her request, we surgically repaired her hip so she wouldn't have to spend her last few weeks or months in bed.

Early the next morning, I was making my rounds on our post-op patients when I headed in to see Emma. There, sitting next to her was her son Brad Anderson. Up until that moment I had never made the connection. He was the only visitor that came to see her for most of the ten days she was there. Two different times I greeted Emma and then asked - "Where's Brad?"

The answers were hard to take in. One day she told me he had an eye doctor's appointment, not at the eye hospital five miles away. It was a couple hours away, because he was already blind in one eye and was starting to lose his vision in the other eye from a very rare disease.

Two days later, she said he was visiting Mr. Anderson in the nursing home. "His father doesn't remember who he is, but he loves to have visitors."

I asked Regina - How could I have possibly been more judgmental and wrong? She responded from her unparalleled vantage point - "Even with suffering, he doesn't have to be bitter."

Regina Set a Very High Bar.

Many of us have heard some variation of - "When we're gone, people won't remember what we've said, they'll remember how we made them feel." That's certainly the case with Regina. She made us feel empowered to make a positive difference and to be grateful for that opportunity.

CHAPTER 42

A New Year's Trip to a Biker's Bar

A couple years ago Brian, my across the street neighbor and motorcycle buddy, asked if I was up for some chicken wings and a beer at a biker bar about half an hour north of us. Not having seen him in a couple months, I was all in. Late the next morning we hopped into his pick-up and were on our way.

We drove through fresh slush past countless farm fields and a couple of semi-frozen lakes. Typically, by mid-December in southern Wisconsin, those lakes are dotted with dozens of locals and out-of-towners vying for crappies, perch and other panfish.

When we got there a little before noon, we were greeted by a Harley right inside the entrance. I'm guessing it met some bare-bones criteria for a biker bar somewhere - thus my alluring title. This Saturday, even though it was packed and quite rowdy, the motorcycle took a back seat to the small-town pool tournament in the back part of the bar.

.

Looking around, there were a couple other motorcycles but no Harley "uniforms," political hats or profanity-laced leather vests anywhere to be had. We fit right in, including a toned-down Brian.

He didn't even have the pistol he typically carries since he was planning on doing some bonding with "Jack." One drink is our limit when on the bikes, so he considers it a safe bet to "carry" then - just in case we run into some intransigent crazies. We've had one discussion on the matter and as Brian is a very levelheaded guy, we've rolled past that one. Somehow, we've become adept at avoiding other issues that are prone to generate heat.

We found two seats at the large oval-shaped bar with a big screen TV and fishing clips staring us down. The well-tattooed waitress in her fifties brought a local IPA for me and a "Jack Daniels and Coke" for Brian. Then we two brothers from another mother continued the conversation we'd started on the way there. We dug deeper than usual since we weren't in a hurry to hop back onto the saddles. Think of gas station - fuel stops, and pee breaks.

We talked about his wife's and his blended family with four guys. And we talked about my two kids and grandkids. Then there were the parenting challenges - mainly our kids' making decisions that to us looked more like learning opportunities than good choices.

And we washed those thoughts down with another round - him ditching the Coke portion because all of a sudden, he'd become a purist. He chased his with chicken wings and I took in my first beef patty of the year. My wife's almost a vegetarian, so in a good week we'll share a dozen shrimp. I was celebrating the New Year.

It sounded like our bar stool neighbors to the left were doing the same. Lots of drinking, and the dice cups were pounding. "Ship, Captain, and Crew" was the game Brian thought they were playing. The guy to my immediate left had at least two Benjamins and a stack of twenties when I first noticed him and the other three players.

About an hour and a half later, after the other three had left, I turned around and asked him, "so how did you do?" His response was - I have no idea. So, I in turn responded - "You don't know whether you're up or down compared to when you started?"

He then offered me my factoid for the day - "It doesn't matter, they're all my friends." And here I was wondering if I had enough in my discretionary fund for another beer.

I remember back in a 2022 reading a poll that about 15% of Americans identified themselves as conservative and are very concerned about political issues. The flip side was also true for liberals. Nobody in that bar was trying to save the world this past Saturday. My hunch is that most of them were in the seventy percent between the two extremes. It was a refreshing break to saddle up within that herd. I 'm just not sure I could afford to go camping with them.

CHAPTER 43

Nothing Lost, Nothing Gained

BE CAREFUL WHERE YOU TREAD,

METAPHORS ARE EVERYWHERE

Over many years of fighting with a worthless, antique GPS, my wife and I had racked up countless wild goose chases, wasted hours on dead end roads, and adventures exploring industrial parks.

My iPhone, though only a few years old, had been inconsistent at best with Google Maps. Emily and I agreed that life was way too short to waste it, going in the wrong direction. So, I did my homework, searched the GPS reviews, found a great deal, and ordered a "new" Garmin. When we got it, I was amazed at how indistinguishable it was from the one we were replacing. . . hmmmm?

We took it for a dry run around our usual haunts, and though it was hard to set up, it got us where we were aiming. Then we took it on its maiden voyage to Lacrosse, WI a couple hours away. It was cooperative until we were in the city and tried to enter the address of the house our friend Kathleen was about to close on. Emily confirmed what she'd written down - "240 Jupiter Street, Lacrosse, Wisconsin," but the GPS kept trying to send us all over the US. I'll admit, there were some harsh words exchanged.

We got so frustrated that in desperation I went to my iPhone to get rescued. I typed in 240 Jupiter Street, and it immediately changed it to 240 *Juniper* Street, Lacrosse. Five minutes later, we pulled into the driveway on JUNIPER Street - the "Sale pending" sign on the front lawn. My phone had a different way of thinking, and for once, we appreciated it.

After the obligatory, though half-hearted apology to our new GPS, we figured we would give it a second chance on the way back to the motel. Emily kept trying to type in 4091 Second Street, Lacrosse, WI . . . but again, to no avail. I decided to give it a try, and having merely typed in 4091 *2nd,* the entire address popped up. We just had to use the language the new friend could relate to.

Both the phone and the new GPS had different skill sets and favorable qualities. We just needed to give them a chance. And maybe cut them a little slack for their weaknesses - we had just demonstrated that we had our own.

CHAPTER 44

An Unforgettable Night

The Intruder

One can never be prepared for the "unthinkable," but I thought I had done my best. We made sure there were various levels of resistance available if our security system was ever breached. From an antique can of spray deodorant to my son's old aluminum baseball bat stowed away in our closet, I thought we had the bases covered.

But in hindsight, no amount of planning for the worst-case scenario would have gotten me prepared for last night. I had checked the locks on both doors before bed, and they were still locked this morning. All the locks on the downstairs windows had been latched. Echoes of, "it'll never happen to me," ironically bounced around my head as I confirmed again that we hadn't set ourselves up for disaster.

I reflected on the fact that old adages such as, "bad things don't happen to good people," was just crazy talk. I'd merely gotten up to pee. I heard nothing unusual. And I saw nothing unusual, though it was mighty dark - in more ways than one as it turns out.

I did my deed and then washed my hands while silently singing "Happy Birthday to Me," as my grandkids learned to do during the pandemic. The song apparently takes about twenty seconds, which is how long the mightiest Corona virus can hold on before giving up their fight.

In retrospect, I guess I was singing myself back to sleep because I was completely caught off guard by what happened next. Mind you, I feel guilty even mentioning all of this because I know there are so many people that have suffered far worse in their lives. But for me here in my highly sheltered environment, it doesn't take much to rock a boat.

My wife was sleeping a mere fifteen feet away from a crime scene and never even stirred as my nightmare unfolded. Evidently, she's not as woke as my conservative relatives might think.

Anyway, I had just finished washing my hands and had turned on the faucet so I could add just a little water to one of those blue metal camping mugs. You know the ones we see on the LL Bean tent ads. I couldn't see the blue, but I knew it was there - unlike the evil that lurked within my very bathroom.

With no hint of suspicion, I raised the cup to my lips. It was then that I felt the searing pain. Maybe it was a little biting in character but certainly of a degree that the world has never known. My imagination went wild, but simultaneously all my neurons kicked into overdrive - and I not only saved my wife, but I became a real man in the process!

With lightning speed, I took a blind swipe and turned on the light. I stood there for a fleeting second staring into the cold beady eyes of the intruder. . . and somehow harnessing limitless resources, I threw open the sash and tossed that bastard right out our second story window!

And the Moral of the Story - - -

No earwig is ever going to pinch the lip of a guy from South Jersey and live to talk about it!

BTW - The story about the pinching earwig, and the blue metal cup that it was in - was indeed true, *but like so many of the stories that we encounter, there's a kernel of truth - dramatized, embellished and distorted to make some dubious point.*

CHAPTER 45

A N G E R T A I N M E N T

Claiming Countless Lives

A DEMON HAS TAKEN HOLD OF ME.

A couple years ago, as I was working on dinner, I couldn't find my favorite, semi-flat strainer and I needed it pronto. As I thrashed around the kitchen, I remembered my wife had left it behind in NY, as we raced westward. I vented to myself - "Come on - it's an oversized spoon, not some Cuisinart Mixer" I was unreasonably angry and found myself getting nasty to my bride over a measly' cooking utensil - but not really.

Half an hour earlier, I was sifting through lots of news on the computer from CNN to Fox, from MSNBC to BBC. Beer in hand, I read for the hundredth time that Trump might be indicted . . . and I read for the hundredth time that the investigations were politically motivated, inferring that he had done nothing illegal.

I read how Putin made a deal to station nukes in Belarus. And I saw again how so many people were suffering immeasurably on both sides of the Russia-Ukraine war. I was very angry at the injustice and insane amounts of needless misery.

AND THAT, IS WHY I WAS PISSED

It's certainly not a novel problem and it's happening all over our state, country, and world. Whether it's manifest on our nation's highways or the back alleys of our cities, at CEO board meetings or across the kitchen table, that anger is taking us to bad places.

And most of us are victims - to one degree or other. Fear and anger all too often turn to rage, and that all but guarantees continued engagement. The grand prize winners are TV ratings and stockholders, which translates to raises and obscenely rich people getting even richer at the expense of most working families. That anger and division also keep us from even touching on the underlying causes of complex societal problems

As I mentioned a couple chapters ago, roughly 30% of Americans are deeply invested in politics - that's a lot of people being stoked daily! There's a fine line between being current and being supersaturated with news. Consider for one minute the percentage of news stories that you've encountered in the last twenty-four hours that are *both new and significant*. I dare say very few.

SO, WHAT IS AN ANGERTAINMENT JUNKEE TO DO?

First, we could start by acknowledging that we have a serious problem that is toxic to everyone within our circles, especially to those we love. We could admit that we are willing participants in this, and not innocent bystanders. After facing these facts, we could stop paying our cable bills, drive the car over our cell phones, shoot the computer, and drop our TV remotes in the sharp's containers at a public restroom.

OR . . . my advice to fellow addicts.

As is the case with so many other <u>self-induced</u> mental health issues, we could exercise some discipline. We could set limits, which is very easily done! The tough part is working out those limits in such a way that they're both doable and sustainable.

My personal limits are simple – I'm "allowed" to check the main news feed headlines, without the commentary, once each morning. If there is anything of major consequence or new, I can spend ten minutes reading about it from opposing sides – 99% of the time I'm done in ten minutes, and a much happier camper in the process!

And then, take frequent "vacations" outside our head – examples might be - sports, hobbies, church, volunteer work, or socializing with healthier peers or our kids and grandkids if we've been so blessed.

Speaking of church, we could grab on to a mantra or phrase that helps us move to a better place. One of my favorites that I memorized years ago is - "Whatever is true, honorable, just, whatever is pure, lovely, or gracious, where there be any excellence, where there be anything worthy of praise, think upon these things." (Philippians 4:8)

AND, we could fraternize with the *perceived* "enemy" - those from the other camp. They are not our enemy, as we're repeatedly led to believe. When we realize "those people" are fundamentally more like us than not, it just might take some of the wind out of both of our sails.

CHAPTER 46

Today is Apparently My Last Day
(A Bit Fictionalized)

It was a typical night that started like any other.

I had just rolled into another round of deep sleep, when I heard an angelic voice and got a faint visual. It was that of our long-lost neighbor, Eva. Though she had died ten years earlier, she looked good, but her words were anything but good.

"Mark, I'm so sorry to wake you with bad news, but today is your last day." And then she added her signature "but I know it's going to be all right."

In an instant, she vanished. Even though she was one of the kindest, most down-to-earth people I'd ever met, her words were downright creepy! Never having had a premonition before, I tried to let it go.

But it ended up taking me hours of tossing and turning to get back to any semblance of sleep. On some level I knew I was dreaming, but still so happy to be hooking into one of my old hang-gliders again.

I stood, taking in the breeze at the top of the mountain. I'd just started to charge down the twenty-foot ramp to get up to flying speed, when out of nowhere came my long-gone mother's voice - "Don't forget your seatbelt, I'll see you soon." I sat bolt upright in bed and found myself shaking. I quietly got up, and in a trance, walked to the bathroom.

Even the mirror looked ominous. After what seemed like hours of consternation, I finally got back to sleep, only to be awakened by my long-dead father's startling yell - "Get the hell out of bed - don't you dare waste this day!"

Somehow my wife managed to stay asleep despite my turbulent and terrifying night. I had more than a sneaking suspicion that I was going to die – on that day.

Well, I didn't. But for one glorious day, I lived like I was going to.

CHAPTER 47

Asking Why Can Change
A Trajectory

Unpleasant or traumatic experiences can certainly help shape our futures, but do they have to define us? That's an age-old question with significant implications regarding so many facets of the "US against Them" paradigm.

I'd like to share my thoughts regarding an unpleasant experience I had decades ago. Although it was relatively trivial on a scale of things, a wrong choice on my part or my brothers could have led to the destruction of several lives.

One Christmas night when I was a senior in high school, my family went to a party at my aunt and uncle's house. It was about five miles from ours, and for a reason I can't recall, I couldn't go with them. After some walking, I turned onto a four-mile stretch of a two-lane road. And I got a "bright" idea. I could put my thumb out!

I had heard somewhere that hitch hiking was dangerous, but this was Christmas, the celebration of the birth of "The Prince of Peace."

Those were my thoughts as I entered the all-black town. Within ten minutes, as I was crossing a bridge over the interstate to Philadelphia, I saw two guys approaching. They were a little older than me and one of them was looking down at me, from a distance.

The authoritative figure stated that they "just needed bridge money to go to Philly," seven miles away. I'd seen enough movies and cop shows to know that this was just a ploy to get me to pull out my wallet. Since it contained a five-dollar bill, I didn't reach into my back pocket. But I did explain, "I don't have any money for the bridge," all the while watching the big guy in case he made his move.

Their heads pivoted back and forth as they watched the rare car pass by and eyed the guardrail and traffic below. This all happened over the course of maybe two minutes. They were considering their options, and I was working through mine when the smaller guy sucker punched me on the side of the head. I wasn't knocked down but was doing a momentary regroup as a car came careening toward us. With tires screeching, it stopped only a few feet away.

I do believe it had the desired effect as I was able to run past the car, and both guys ran off in the opposite direction. At no time did I come close to seeing who rescued me, but a fleeting glance told me it wasn't a police car. I ran until I couldn't and then walked the rest of the way to the party.

It so happens that my older brother had spent much of his last year as a Marine in the rice patties of Vietnam. I was still in the afterglow of having him back with us, alive and almost well. While we were alone talking, he sensed something was off with me and asked, "Are you alright?" So, I explained what had happened to his little brother.

Stiffening up he asked, "Do you want to go find them?" My response was apparently too casual as I said, "sure," and made some reference to fighting. I still remember his words and an intensity that I'd never witnessed from anyone. "If you wanna fuckin' kill 'em, let's go, but I'm not gonna go play."

And, we never talked about it again.

Only one path led to a better place, and that was putting the incident behind me. For some reason, the minimally traumatic experience never got a chance to fester. Most recently I questioned, had I let it go, or was I merely suppressing it?

On reflection, I realized that it was in my "file box" where I could retrieve it, but I just never chose to. Of all the regrets I've had in my life, it didn't even register.

I have never harbored animosity toward those guys, or "their kind." It's certainly not because I have thick skin or I'm a bad-ass - I don't, and I'm not.

So, what *is* the deal?

Could it be as simple as – I dug into the question - WHY?

I'm not going to pretend that I can recall what my thoughts were half a century ago. I do think I would have noticed and wondered about the difference between the way people like me lived, and the way that people, unlike me, lived. It didn't take a college education to notice that none of the houses that

I saw in the black neighborhoods were as nice as ours, or our neighbors.

Why was that?

Could it be that all of "Them" were lazy or ignorant, and all of "Us" were smart and ambitious? I knew better. Could it be that "those people" had problems with drugs and alcohol, unlike my people? Definitely not! Personal observations revealed that my clan had more than our fair share of dysfunction - and I didn't even have to step beyond our property line to find it.

Why was it that almost all the black people I saw working, were doing so in the service industry - cleaning rooms in motels, washing dishes or cars, doing janitorial work or cleaning houses, including our own? We had a maid named Mabel for a couple years, and she worked every bit as hard or harder than my mother did. Why was that?

My father had a job shop, contracting out engineers and draftsmen to do relatively short-term projects for different industries or the military. Though he certainly *didn't* keep his generic distain for "colored people," a secret, he really opened my eyes one day.

I don't remember the context, but I believe he said, "If I have to choose between two men to send for a job and they have exactly the same qualifications and education, I will always send the colored guy. I know he had to work twice as hard as

the white guy to get to the same spot in life."
Why was that?

I am certainly not trying to excuse criminal behavior; but I am trying to understand where it came from. There are more ways than one to address societal problems.

Who knows? Maybe just asking the question "why" could change the way we process, store and grow from our encounters or experiences.

CHAPTER 48

A Flying Experience & Life Lesson

For as long as I can remember I've been mesmerized by soaring birds...and airplanes.

I had a few short and long-term goals which grew from my roots in a small town in New Jersey. Becoming an Eagle Scout, a private pilot, and then an Air Force pilot were at the top of my list, and I spent the lion's share of my time and money working toward those goals. As it turned out, my two irregularly shaped eyeballs were good enough for the first two goals but a deal-breaker for the third. Regardless, flying has remained a life-long passion.

Flying in its most basic form is a Zen-like experience. Many consider it a sure-fire way to get above and beyond all that ails we earthlings. Pragmatically speaking, it's also fairly safe. Pilots rarely die while they're flying - it's typically when they stop flying!

And that is what I almost did fifteen years ago! I had a Dacron and aluminum - "Skycycle." It is basically a hang-glider with a small motorcycle engine spinning a wooden prop a thousand times a minute. Having just taken off, I was in a steep climb when a wire connection broke, and that screaming engine went silent in a microsecond - fifty feet above the runway!

Any unpowered flying device with its nose up in the air will drop like an anvil if its forward momentum doesn't provide enough lift through the wings. I immediately yanked the control bar in, pointing the nose toward the ground to pick up airspeed. And then, maybe a second later, threw the bar out to flare into a landing - barely escaping a catastrophe.

The total "flight time" was under 10 seconds!

Most of us are familiar with some rendition of the "fight or flight" reaction. The above misadventure exemplifies what an analogous neurological response looks like on a good day. That would be when training, conditioning, and divine intervention join forces to save someone's butt. Any time we have a close call in life, there's the temptation to let it leave a disproportionately large dent in our spirit.

Whether that bad experience has to do with flying, sports, or a clash in relationships, we have the option to first chill and then reflect. Defaulting to "I'm never going to do that again" might make sense on some level but, it's dangerously close to "all done."

Sometimes we get so stuck in the emotional response to a situation that we end up residing there, indefinitely immersed in its paralysis.

When we lose our objectivity, or our ability to step outside our emotions to solve problems, we run the risk of fearing life itself and that could mean -

NEVER SOARING AGAIN!

CHAPTER 49

As We are Fully Known

Four Lambeau Field football stadiums worth of people are having their very worst day ever – TODAY!

Per my math and aggregates of numbers which I've put together, there are roughly 8 billion of us on this planet and each of us lives an average of 26,645 days. Since every individual has a worst day, that amounts to roughly 300,244 people having their absolute worst day – right now as you're reading this!

"On Their Worst Day"

I've met lots of men, women, and children because of their worst day ever. Many of them are disabled US veterans who sacrificed so much for what they believed in - and for us.

Through my work in a couple of refugee camps, I've also met numerous Vietnamese and Nicaraguans because of their worst days - as they left their families, everything they own, and their homelands.

In an ideal world, the worst part of anyone's life wouldn't necessarily define them, but amazingly good and bad legacies have come out of these tragic life - shaping experiences.

One of the most "disabled" veterans I've ever worked with or for, was U.S Army Staff Sergeant (Ret.) Travis Mills who described having "had a bad day at work" April 10, 2012. He left various portions of all four extremities in Afghanistan. But I use the term disabled inappropriately here.

He's probably done more good in his lifetime, since his injuries than most of us will ever do. I met him and his wife in Maine at the headquarters of their non-profit called the Travis Mills Foundation. While there, I helped with adaptive winter sports for many other severely injured vets. There were the usual outward signs of their injuries - like wheelchairs, heavy scars and prostheses, but the injuries don't stop where the clothing starts.

There are millions of other war veterans across the US and around the world whose scars are not so visible. Most of them also sacrificed for what they thought to be the greater good. And not all of them look like you or me.

And then there are the countless victims of violence of every type - whose worst day never really ends.

Maximum security prisons are filled with people who will pay for the bad choices they've made - on their worst day. We've all had bad days, but some have had particularly bad days that "keep on giving."

192

Few of us can accurately imagine what the best or worst day of another person really looked like. But the better we know them, and the more we understand them, the closer we'll get.

I Know a Guy - we'll call him "Steve."

He is one of my best friends, but he would never think so. Why? Because we're so different politically and in terms of some of our values. Most of my overtures to reconnect have been ignored at best. However, a deeper dive reveals that we've lived through a lot of the same chaos together and each made more than our fair share of mistakes. I know we've hurt and at times disappointed each other.

And I still have great memories from when the bonds were strong. Like the one when we were wrestling in the back yard and I threw him - resulting in a long smear of fresh dog pooh the length of his back. And then there was the Florida trip two decades ago when I, as a relative motorcycle newbie, drove his 800-pound Harley Road Glide for the first time – with him on the back!

Despite all the above, I still can't fathom what his worst days were like as a Marine in Vietnam. I know he's at heart, a very loving, kind, generous, and creative person. It must have been painful beyond all measure for him.

I can only say this because I knew him *before* his worst days, the ones that disproportionately shaped the rest of my brother's life.

CHAPTER 50

Knee-jerks and Unintended Consequences

A Cat Exploited for Metaphorical Purposes

Recently I had a humbling experience. On my way to the coffee maker for my wake-up charge, I spotted a large cat slithering down our shaded driveway. Noticing that it looked well fed, my gut screamed - YOU are not going to eat another bird - at least in my yard! Having recently resorted to spending a couple hundred bucks on a deer and squirrel-proof bird feeder, the last thing I wanted was a cat neutering that investment.

So, I angrily slammed the back of my fist against the side door and the feline darted.

But then, it occurred to me that I'd never seen that specific cat before. And to make matters worse, I then recalled seeing a notice about a missing cat a few days ago. So, I ran out to offer it some cheese, but it was too late.

The cat did not like or trust me. And I'd never given it a chance to - nor vice versa!

I had raced into conclusions which were devoid of facts - and stuffed that likely innocent furball into my old "enemy file."

One would think that I would have known better. I can only hope that the next time I'll think first before misfiling a new encounter – with or without the oversized canines.

CHAPTER 51

Just Showing Up Is Not Enough

Decreasing the divide between Us and Them requires at least a rudimentary understanding of "Them," and that starts with an open mind and some serious listening.

Photo courtesy of "Road Trip with Raj" © - Unsplash

Most of us have been there - we're at a friend's holiday party or sizable work gathering when in walks a guy we've never seen before. Maybe his nose seems a bit inclined toward the ceiling as he scans the room. When he starts to fumble with his cell phone, it dawns on you that he probably doesn't know anyone here. You decide to be welcoming and walk over to introduce yourself.

He's still scanning the room as you approach, even though you're now five feet in front of him. You look up slightly to catch his eyes, but that's not happening.' He somehow manages to look right through you. As you commit to engage him, he turns toward the side and glances out the window toward the trash cans. And it's those dented, rusted vessels of nothingness that return a most appropriate glance.

The dude has told you six ways to Sunday that he is not interested in talking with you, and yet not one word was spoken. How did he so knowingly do that, and have we ever done the same?

So, What Just Happened?

First off, as you read the scenario above, did you find yourself judging, either the new guy or the person approaching him? I found myself judging the unfriendly jerk, and I was the one who created him.

Right out of the starting gate, I had a bias because I'm more of an extrovert and tend to see social interactions from that perspective. I never even considered the possibility that the guy might be an introvert or dealing with some social anxiety.

How would it have changed if I had given a description of the new guy? What about his age, or how he was dressed? How about if he was instead, she? Skin color? What if I described seeing "Autism Speaks" emblazoned on his shirt? Imagine that he was wearing a pair of sunglasses at an evening party.

So much could and maybe should be taken into consideration before we even take our first step in this scenario. Once we make our move, we unfortunately emit non-verbal signals like pheromones from a feral cat. Despite our best intentions, we might have made this bashful guy quite uncomfortable.

In my earlier chapters on engaged listening, I addressed the importance of being intentional and respectful. Today, I'll add the importance of paying attention to non-verbal cues - coming or going. Maybe the first part of respecting someone is respecting their space. Some people may not even welcome a "Hello," let alone an actual conversation with a stranger.

Now, just for kicks and giggles, let's imagine that instead of the new guy turning toward the window as you approach, he offers a relatively meek "Hi," in response to yours. You've broken the ice. Introducing yourself with a firm, though non–pain inducing handshake, you've sent a clear message and it's a chance for him to send his. Since there's good eye contact as he responds in kind, you're actually off to a good start.

After a few pleasantries are exchanged, you realize this guy is new to the area - and becoming more at ease. He's certainly not threatening. You notice that he's looking directly at you and yet avoiding the intimidating stare. You've gleaned that you have a couple of things in common - so the conversation is now less strained and has become interesting.

As you're talking, you get a text, and seeing that it's not urgent, you apologize and silence the phone in front of him. That is the twenty-first century equivalent of tipping your hat and bowing. It is a disproportionately large signal of respect, and it cannot be overrated.

So much of non-verbal communication amounts to letting the other party know that you are fully present. Eliminating as many distractions as possible is a good place to start. For example, pivoting your position may be necessary to avoid being distracted by news as it scrolls by on the screen behind your conversation partner. Turning down the music in the background conveys that this conversation is important to you, and who wouldn't welcome that overture?

Periodic appropriate gestures and subtle head nods may also let that partner know you're paying attention, whether or not you're in agreement. Even one's posture and shoulder position may confer boredom or interest.

All the above-mentioned factors add up like vectors and influence the overall direction the conversation is likely to take. You are not an innocent bystander, but a participant in something that could leave you both in a better place.

CHAPTER 52

American Roots - Immigrants & Grit

Each one of us are the sum total of so many variables. Genetics, upbringing, support systems, information feeds, life experiences - they all play their part. But it's the choices we make along our path that have an over-sized role in determining who we are and where we go with our lives.

Since Emily, my wife, left on her "great adventure" this past winter, I've been forced to make more substantive choices than usual. We are, after all - only young once and coasting to the finish line is not an appealing option for me.

In addition, Emily did leave her mark on me. Notoriously soft-spoken, she was also fearless in so many ways. She would readily admit that there were dangerous creeps "out there," but would spend more time praying for their tortured souls than worrying about them.

I still hear echoes of her - "what we fill our minds with, we attract."

Fall is in the air- all photos by Mark VL

With the above thoughts in mind, I've made two recent investments. One, a steel vault to lock up all my "but what ifs," and the other, a ten-foot, used RV trailer - called a Scamp.

My plan, at least while I'm unattached, is to spread my wings a bit and take in a serious infusion of nature. Just as importantly, I'd like to make connections and dispel myths - my own and those of others. What are those people so "unlike me," really like, and what food for thought can we exchange?

After a somewhat frenzied lift off from my hometown, I headed north about an hour's drive to a Wisconsin State campground. Settling in took a while since I'm a backpacker at heart and everything about RV-camping is new to me. Camping had lost its appeal for Emily years ago, so this was one of the "silver linings" I was able to fly through as I moved forward.

View from my $25 per night campsite

The campground was remarkably peaceful, and maybe one quarter full, so I spent the first two days peddling the State Park's roads, hiking the trails, and swimming all around the beautiful lake pictured above. The ever-present mosquitos were there to remind me that this was just a knock-off of heaven, not the real thing.

The second night was one to remember. After eating my warmed-up beef stroganoff, I set off on my mountain bike to explore prospects for a potential winter camp site. Within 200 feet, I realized that my current campsite did not offer the best view of the sunset. It turns out a guy named "Omar" had an even more dynamite view of the departing sun!

After our introductions, this pleasant, twenty-five-year-old guy was quick to admit that this was his first night camping in the woods - ever! In fact, he had had his new camping gear over-nighted from Amazon two days prior to me meeting him. He was glad to learn that I was another solo camper, but he gave a measured and kind response when I explained why. He had attempted to get some of his friends to join him, but he only got one "maybe" for his efforts.

The following is to the best of my recollection, but I did omit several personal stories - respecting Omar and his family's privacy. He did, however, give me permission to pass along his story. Incidentally, his English was pristine, and with no discernible accent.

Omar was a most gracious host. He put a hot dog on his only skewer and had held it over the campfire a couple minutes when he acknowledged - "I have no idea how you like your hot dogs - here, why don't you finish it." Then, as he added a log to the fire, he asked if I'd be interested in a beer or a "Jack & Pepsi."

I accepted the latter, which set us off on a deep dive into so many areas of substance. "Thanks," I responded. "I am fine with both of us drinking alcohol, but I'm a bit surprised that you are also. I guess I had assumed that you were a Muslim." He went on to explain that yes, he was, but not a "practicing" Muslim.

My thoughts wandered to all the people who self-identified as Christians and yet hid their piety so well. I explained that I'd gotten slower to criticize the religious beliefs of others as mine have morphed over the years. For me, how people treat each other and the planet which our great grandchildren will inherit - has taken a front pew to what people say they believe.

This photo is of the confluence of our
moon and Venus during a pre-dawn walk at the lake.

.

Though Omar was born in Baghdad, he spent a large portion of his earliest years traveling with his sister and parents, as they tried to escape the violence in Iraq and its war-torn neighbors.

His father in particular bore an unfathomable load (including 18 days of torture) as they worked their way from country to country toward Syria, where he and his sister attended middle school. As he shared the journey, he pointed to the tattoo on his upper arm in memory of his endeared younger brother who died while in Iraq.

The conversation drifted toward his arrival here in the US, his time at the University of Wisconsin where he earned a degree in psychology, and the jobs he'd held since. But two positions caught my attention.

With his charismatic personality I was not surprised that he was a successful car salesman, and he was rightfully proud to have sold three vehicles on one very memorable day.

But what really impressed me was his reason for leaving that lucrative work. He explained that, for every sizable profit he was able to finagle through a sale, there was a comparable financial loss for the customer . . . "I just couldn't live with that."

With that explanation, I was emboldened to challenge him on his - not being a "practicing Muslim'. It could be a coincidence but both he and a Muslim physician that I'd worked with decades ago, emanated strong ethics when it came to not profiting at another's expense.

Having gone on to study criminal justice, his current work was that of a corrections officer. He floated between shifts at the medium and maximum-security prisons where he seemed to like the challenges of his work. I had to cut him off as he worked his way through a long list of the unfathomable things that his inmates had done to earn their guaranteed life sentences. Omar pointed out that merely showing the men some respect as fellow humans - was a gift he could offer.

He spoke very highly of the family with whom he lived. He shared how his mother had always been his best friend, and how his father for instance made certain that his breakfast and uniforms were prepared for him each workday. It was a joy to see him light up as he talked about the woman he'd loved for several years who'd recently become his fiancée.

Over the course of our conversation, he excused himself several times as family members, including a cousin in Iraq, called to check in on him. They were mostly carried out in Arabic and there was a lot of smiling and laughing. He also learned that one of his "maybe" fellow campers was on his way.

Zachariah showed up around 10 PM and was interesting in his own right. Coming from Kenya he immigrated to America about the same time as Omar did. He had a passion for long-distance running and was employed as a registered nurse. He shared how he really wanted to learn more about medicine, maybe on his way to becoming a nurse practitioner. I'm sure I could have listened to him for hours as well, but having gotten up around five, it was time for my mind to take a rest and then start processing.

So, where does that leave me ten days out? It leaves me wishing that I'd had another couple days to flesh out the narratives of these two young men. But it also leaves me grateful for the opportunity to take in, firsthand, the story of someone - so unlike myself. That experience has reinforced my sense that immigration reform is every bit as complex as each of the million people who struggle to make their way across our borders each year.

CHAPTER 53

Small Choices and Cliffs

I know I've alluded to the fact that I was a small guy in middle school, but the contrast versus "normal sized kids" grew worse as I entered high school.

My family had recently moved to Cherry Hill, NJ, a sprawling suburb of Philly. I timidly walked through one of the countless glass doors of my new school at five feet and 80 pounds. No one would have ever considered me intimidating.

That would have been Jim Ford, another new freshman. He wasn't a particularly large guy, but he came from the big city. As an older freshman, he arrived via one of Philadelphia's juvenile detention centers after getting caught for "breaking and entering." He had apparently targeted the wrong house and left a blood trail and the end of his pinky as he escaped through a broken window.

We were both on the fringes and basically loners until we discovered each other. Wildly contrasting stories were shared, and new ones generated. He was fun to be with, gutsy and adventurous, but Jimmy certainly wasn't wholesome. And he never spoke of his family.

Late one night, we were walking across a vacant parking lot when a town cop drove toward us. I don't remember what we had been up to, but I'm sure it wasn't covertly planting flowers at the nearby nursing home. As he pulled up next to us, I "nonchalantly" slid my over-sized switchblade beneath his car. He didn't consider it very slick and had me crawl under the patrol car to retrieve it.

There were a few questions asked, followed by a short discussion of our options. He decided to spare us the part where our parents would pick us up at the station. The knife became his and the lesson-learned was mine. Though it was a miniscule incident, it hit me as a wakeup call. I realized that as part of our developing friendship, I'd taken too many steps up a dead-end road and the red lights were flashing.

I was blessed with an ambitious, well-principled father who happened to be a huge fan of corporal punishment. I had a loving mother, three siblings, and an extended family who I didn't want to disappoint. And, I had a bunch of kind, supportive Boy Scout leaders who had high hopes for me.

Most importantly, I had attainable goals within reach. Not everyone is so blessed.

CHAPTER 54

Better Communication Equals Judging Less and Listening More

"How can we become less judgmental when we listen?" I personally would answer that question with another question. If I had spent even the last twenty-four hours in the shoes of the person in front of me, would I be thinking more like them?

During conversations, it's almost natural to fall into judgement. That would be the process whereby we assess how well another person seems to be doing or thinking - based on our gifts and talents, upbringing, education, resources, and experiences. We are unique, as are the ways we critique or assimilate information.

That being said, curiosity combined with a focused effort, can nudge us away from judging and toward a better understanding. Sometimes requesting clarification such as - "Please help me understand how you came to that conclusion," can go a long way toward respectful discourse.

More times than not, just adding "tell me more" can further elevate the levels of the conversation and be quite educational. Some individuals have been trained from an early age to accept, without questioning, anything they've been told by authoritative figures. Is it surprising that those same people might gravitate toward tiered structures of authority such as conservative churches, the military, or law enforcement? It is in those environments where scrutinizing information delivered from on high, is rarely tolerated, much less encouraged. That's where dissenting thoughts are often considered heresy, and fact-checking an unknown or radical concept.

Along the same vein, some people are just more comfortable assimilating the thoughts of others than generating thoughts of their own. These well-intentioned people may be particularly vulnerable to sophisticated, agenda-driven truth-spinners.

Occasionally I encounter those whose only approach to addressing complex topics is to reel off over-simplified and meaningless talking points. In that situation, I have to step back and remind myself - If I were drawn to a place where I was fed only marshmallows, day in and day out, my brain would be fluffy too.

CHAPTER 55

Saved by a Duck Lady & Company

There is no way that any of us could ever anticipate the turn of events that would play out on any given day.

Author at Devil's Lake - "Balanced Rock"

I'd spent the first day of October exploring the majestic bluffs that lined the eastern side of Devil's Lake here in Wisconsin. I then hiked down around the southern tip of the mile-long lake to the western side, where an enormous boulder field cascaded down the steep slope. Between the vistas, interesting conversations and countless large birds soaring the bluffs, it was a Grade "A" Day - but I doubt I'll remember much of it a year from now.

The next day was a different story. I'd ridden my bike down from the campground where I was staying. I headed to "our spot" along the lake for a long swim. My late wife Emily and I sat on the same shoreline rocks near a *tiny island* -a year earlier - taking in the beautiful view while trying to process her dismal prognosis. It turned out to be our last weekend vacation together and I wanted to commemorate the occasion. She'd come along for the ride in my backpack.

Having locked my bike to a nearby tree, I was stuffing the half-cup container into my swim trunks as a low-flying turkey vulture pierced the bright sky above. Though I would have liked to have been "in the moment," I couldn't help but be distracted by a young woman and an older grey-haired guy on that island of sand fifty yards away.

Note the small island at 3 o'clock

In her mid-thirties, the brunette kept harassing a pair of ducks. From what I could hear and her tone, it seemed that she thought the two mallards had just flown in from a different planet. "Come to Mama . . . don't go over there, that's not safe . . . stay here . . . come to mama, there are some minnows here." It sounded like she'd even named them. To make matters worse, the bearded guy, maybe her father, just stood there humoring her.

Trying to put all that behind me, I started swimming upwind toward the center of the lake. As the chattering in the background slowly disappeared, I realized that the tightness around my bathing suit pocket had also disappeared - the container was gone!

I checked a complete circle around me and then started diving, almost reaching the bottom, maybe ten feet away. The water was fairly clear, but unfortunately, so was the container with the exception of the tan lid. Emily was a free spirit. The last thing I wanted was for her to be confined to a tub of plastic at the bottom of a lake. Or even worse, to end up as "garbage" discovered next year along the shoreline.

So, I kept looking, over the course of roughly half an hour searching in ever-widening circles above and below the surface. I worked my way back toward the rocks where I'd left, since there was still a breeze from behind me and I thought Emily might be surfing back to the shore.

And then I heard yelling. "What are you looking for?" It was the duck lady!

Maybe a hundred feet away, I stood up and responded in hushed tones - "Well, it's kind of a covert operation - but I lost my wife, or at least some of her ashes." And thus began our steps into each other's story.

Heather and her deceased father's best friend, Terry, described seeing something floating off in the distance, maybe fifteen minutes earlier. As I was describing the container, Terry searched off into the distance eventually shouting - I think I see it. He directed me as I swam toward the bobbing plastic.
One minute later, I stood off the shore of their little island, waving triumphantly with Emily's ashes in my hand. Without

skipping a beat, Heather pointed out - "there's a Monarch butterfly circling above you!"

I explained that they and all pollinators were my wife's passion. Though I hadn't seen one in months, it wasn't a surprise as I've had so many wonderful "coincidences" since Emily died - some defying any rational explanations.

Heather replied - "I don't doubt you at all. I watched half of my six-year-old son disappear when he was hit by a semi." She went on to say, "since losing him, I've had so many of those types of experiences that I stopped sharing them for fear that people would think I was crazy."

Speaking of which, Heather was not a crazed duck lady. "Tia and Luca" were her two Rouen ducks which she'd been nurturing and training since she bought them from the local - Tractor Supply store two years earlier. She'd met up with Terry at Devil's lake so the four of them could enjoy a day of relaxing on the water - obviously two were more immersed in the experience than the other two.

Feeling much more at ease, I gave my thanks and said my goodbyes. Then I started my swim toward the center of the lake - with container in hand. I hadn't gone a hundred yards when I heard them yelling again. This time, I looked back and saw a half-dozen turkey vultures soaring ever - closer to the two ducks with Terry and Heather trying to protect them and chase the buzzards away.

I opened the cannister and with one swirl, Emily was where she'd forever want to be - free.

The situation on the beach had escalated by the time I raced back. At one point there were twenty-some buzzards all vying for fresh duck - and way too low for comfort. The closest swooped within ten feet of Heather who was screaming at the six-foot birds to "get out of here," and that was only when she wasn't soliciting the help of every deity she'd ever heard of. She might have even thrown some rocks and profanities at the "poor" birds.

Terry and I kept trying to corral her pets to keep them from escaping to open water where they would be even more vulnerable – translation – dead meat.

This situation waxed and waned for more than an hour before there was a slow but mass exodus of the intruders. We parted with some shared gratitude, a hug, and a handshake,

.

Emotional experiences are the ones most likely to steal our hearts or imprint neuronal pathways with tentacle-like extensions, be they based on fact or fiction. It is for those reasons that the second day of October was nothing short of a gift to me.

CHAPTER 56

What do We Sacrifice When We're Wrong?

I've given up on the struggle to stay as fit as a fiddle, but I do strive to stay at least as fit as a ukulele. One of the things that keeps me invested are the occasional, interesting conversations at the gym.

Ater talking to a beekeeper about how his tiny pets were acclimating to the temperature swings from 73 degrees yesterday to 17 degrees this morning, I ended up talking to Ed, a 60ish-year-old guy who I've known for a year or so. Somehow, our discussion drifted toward religion.

I knew, from prior discussions, that he was an atheist, but I had no idea how devout he was. No matter what seemingly open-ended questions I lobbed his way, he spiked every single one down without a thought. "Could you at least consider that there might be some divine mystery out there that we just don't understand?" His reply: "Nah, there isn't any divine anything that we humans didn't create."

Baptized and then raised as a rigid, practicing Catholic, he was as burned out on religion and spirituality as anyone could possibly get. To Ed, the two were the same. He was obviously struggling to squeeze every Christian of every persuasion into the same fundamentalist box. He could not comprehend that all believers weren't close-minded, naive, or just downright ignorant - so . . .

I brought up a personal experience that defied all earthbound explanations, at least for me. I explained how I had an almost universally catastrophic type of hang-glider accident twenty years ago. I was soaring in the Catskill Mountains when a downdraft caught my hang glider, and I flew headfirst into a large tree trunk about sixty feet off the ground. It destroyed the two-inch aircraft aluminum on each side of my head. Though I was powerless in that second, I surprisingly had time to remember the multiple incident reports I'd read about this type of accident; almost universally causing broken necks and fatalities.

As for me, I somehow escaped without a scratch from the impact. My helmet was untouched, and my last visual had been the tree trunk flying toward my face. His immediate response was - "You sure were lucky." My reaction at the time was a confused, but extremely grateful: "Thank you, thank you, thank you, God." I had defied all the odds right there in front of me.

Photo by Alora Griffiths © - Unsplash

Now juxtapose that discussion with one I had with a woman last week.

First, a little background. My wife and I had met "Peggy Sue" as a waitress at a nice pizza place four years earlier. In her early fifties, she seemed pleasant and chatted with us about our recent move to Wisconsin, and eventually about her memorable name. She was a chiropractor but underemployed so that she could take care of her elderly father at his home.

Fast forward three years. We were at the gym and she, not recognizing me, approached and asked if I would spot for her. I said "sure" and stood above her with my hands loosely encircling the bar as she bench-pressed about 140 pounds –a little less than her body weight! When she had finished the set, I introduced myself and said she looked familiar. She gave her name, and the encounter came back to me. So, I asked her how her father was doing. Appearing in a hurry, she gave a casual and bewildered response: "fine."

Well, last week she approached me, and apologized for "again forgetting my name." I tried to reassure her, saying "When you've got a lot on your plate, it's important to let the stuff that doesn't matter fall off." To which she said, "but names do matter." I reminded her that we had met her four years ago when she was waitressing. We talked for a few minutes, including about her father's current health challenge of advanced skin cancer. She asked if I would pray for him to which I gave a sincere "Yes," and then she started to head back to her weights.

Halfway there, she turned around, came back, and asked "Do you accept Jesus as your Lord and savior?" I responded, "That's really complicated, but I will pray for your dad." She wanted nothing of it. The conversation turned from light to intense. She was on a mission. I wasn't sure if she was mainly concerned with saving my soul or doing so in order to make certain that my prayers counted.

First, she started reeling off chapters and verses which I'd heard a hundred times before. She wanted my email address so she could send me information that could "really help" me. I explained that in the last century I was a lay preacher for the Presbyterian church for a decade. I'd thought a lot about all of this, and *we just disagree.* And then I thought I'd wrap things up: "We're in a free country where we're allowed to do that."

She was so far from done. "How about if I send you a link for some videos by a really smart guy who has his doctorate in Biblical history? Can I have your email address?" Now she'd pulled out a piece of paper and a pen. "Can I just take one minute of your time to help you understand?" But she certainly didn't wait for an answer before she dug in. After her third request for my email address, I turned away saying, "No thanks. . . but I'll be praying for your father," thinking to myself: control freaks also need prayers.

Oh, what heavy weights we carry.

CHAPTER 57

A Faulty GPS or Divine Guidance

I really "dislike" driving through large, unfamiliar cities. My word choice here is quite constrained

The part of this driving that I most detest is yielding so much control and the odds of my passenger's survival to an enormously wide array of humanity. It's not that I'm particularly risk averse. But there's such a huge difference between me taking a risk with a substantial benefit in mind and someone else blowing the paint off my front bumper, so they can get home for "the game."

Photography by Thaddaeus Lim© - Unsplash

Such was the case when I was taking Belle, my eight-year-old granddaughter, home after a wonderful visit with my wife and me here in rural Wisconsin. We had entered Milwaukee, and she, in the back seat, was probably two thirds through the book she was reading. It was obviously engaging as she updated me in bursts regarding the on-going saga. The afternoon sun was fading, and a steady rain pelted the windshield.

I had a rough idea of where I was going as I headed toward the northeast side of the city. I'd been to her dad's house several times before, but each time via a different route. Somehow, I lost the Blue Tooth connection with my phone and was forced to rely on Google Map's visual display for confirmation.

Over the course of the sixty-mile trip and several turns, we were still on course and only three miles away from exiting the interstate - when the shit hit the fan. Out of nowhere, the traitorous phone which I held above the steering wheel, commanded that I take the next exit, and I darted to the right thinking my phone's GPS knew something that I didn't. I was very mistaken.

As the rain picked up, I found myself going west instead of east and weaving through multiple lanes of traffic distorted by construction. My sweet Belle kept giving me story updates as the drama unfolded. At one point I asked her to please hold off on the story for just a minute . . . "See those three highways above us, I think we should be on one of them." Obviously, I had a lesson to learn regarding my misplaced priorities because she insisted, "I'm almost done."

With white knuckles, I forced my way over to the first exit that wasn't headed toward another random interstate. After surviving ten minutes in the purgatory, I found myself waiting at a red light. We both noticed a sixtyish-year-old man standing there in the median strip ahead. His only protection from the rain on this fifty-degree day was a worn-out sweatshirt. He held an illegible cardboard sign. As I was thrashing through the center console, the light turned green. I just managed to hand him a five along with a feeble suggestion - "try to keep the faith."

And we were on our way. "Belle," drenched with innocence asked, "Why was he there?"

I said something like - he doesn't have a house like we do and he's hoping people will give him money so he can buy something to eat. And then the kicker - "But what will he do tonight?" The best I could come up with was "hopefully he'll find a piece of dry cardboard somewhere and maybe a bridge to sleep under."

I never heard the end of Belle's story, nor was there another word mentioned about the older man's plight. The quiet emanating from the back seat was painful. I can only imagine that she will be marred by this childhood experience. But, if she's anything like her mother, she'll likely grow from the experience, meld the gifts she's been given with action, and resist the temptation to let the memory fade into the rearview mirror.

CHAPTER 58

Wilma's Legacy

We have been beating each other over the head with ever-improved sticks since the first stick was invented . . . and we can blame it all on Fred.

According to the "Live Sea Scrolls" which I discovered and then burned; the first Fred came upon the first Wilma about umpteen years ago. And they were cool with each other. But that changed one day when Wilma challenged Fred. "Why are you still beating that neighbor over the head with a stick? We now have all the food, water and land that we need."

Fred was very big and very strong, and his response that day was: "BUT I WANT MORE!" Come to think of it, he knew very few words, so that was his response to most of her questions. There was obviously a victim here - and he was nameless. Fred refused to let Wilma even learn his name. He claimed that merely knowing that the "other guy" had a name, would weaken his resolve.

Well, victims don't always stay victims. The other guy, between beatings, was scheming. Ya see, he always wanted more too. Since he wasn't big or strong, he wasn't just thinking; he was inventing.

He revolutionized Fred's stick design. He took a piece of his grapevine and attached a big rock to the end opposite the handle. It was with this most modern device that he slayed Fred one night as he slept. And "Brutus" dragged Wilma back to his cave, kicking and screaming - and he had more!

Over many thousands of years, very little has changed - but the sticks have gotten progressively bigger. Those who can't acquire the largest of sticks just use their smaller sticks with unparallelled brutality.

Thus, it has been, and apparently always will be . . . unless we can learn from the Ghost of Wilma. Her soft voice can still be heard echoing through the hills -

"How's that workin' for ya Fred?"

CHAPTER 59

Elements of Greatness

Photography by Steve Leisher - courtesy Unsplash

The slogan "Make America Great Again" may be catchy, but it ignores a complex reality. It alludes to a time when we as a nation were superb, but there's certainly no broad consensus as to when that would have been. Whichever time was great for some, was invariably horrendous for others.

From our country's earliest days, for every substantial winner, there have always been countless losers. As the European colonists made their push across that which would become our lower 48 states, Native Americans were virtually exterminated. Lest we forget, conquering nations always leave trails of multi-generational suffering.

The same could be said for the hundreds of thousands of blacks brought here like livestock to provide generations of free labor to wealthy settlers. The effects of their denigration and abuse continue to this day.

Unfortunately, there has never been an era in which all of America thrived. However, our nation has been rightfully celebrated for its continued struggle to provide liberty, justice, and opportunity for all.

When any American makes personal sacrifices for the welfare of others - we grow. Every time citizens forgo what they want, so that others are more likely to get what they need, our country evolves. Each time someone stands with a dry mouth and sweaty palms to speak truth to power about inequality and someone else's suffering, we're witnessing elements of greatness.

And when we courageously leave the security of long-held beliefs or political allegiances to vote for a more compassionate and sustainable future for our children and those of our distant neighbors, we nourish greatness.

232

CHAPTER 60

Debriefing

From a New Poll Worker

Photography by Joshua Woroniecki - Unsplash

As of April 2, 2024, my wife and I joined the ranks of our local election poll workers with first rights to the stories thereof.

Before I describe a couple of the more noteworthy experiences, let's talk about the small hoops we had to jump through for the privilege of participating in this pillar of democracy – true and fair elections.

A month earlier, my wife, two other locals, and I took the two-hour long training session for new poll workers - under our city clerk.

As registered voters, that city official knew which political party we represented, and it became obvious from the questions that the two other guys asked, that they were from the opposing party. This was consistent with the balance the election officials strive for in their "election inspectors."

Over the course of twelve pages of handouts and maybe fifty slides, it became abundantly clear that the election process is extremely well thought out. Systems of checks, balances, and redundancy have evolved to the point where undetected election fraud is extremely rare. Many scenarios were presented in which typically unintentional mistakes are made. We were then cautioned as to how to minimize the likelihood that they would occur. And then finally, we were educated as to how the system snags those "mistakes" whether intentional or not.

After completing our classwork, I followed up with my own on-line research regarding actual convictions for election fraud here in my home state. It was relatively fruitless. According to "Wisconsin Watch," - From 2012-2022, "Wisconsin district attorneys brought fewer than 200 cases, the equivalent of 0.0006% of votes cast — with a voter's probation status as the most common reason."

Contrary to disinformation widely disseminated, actual intentional election fraud cases, leading to prosecution, probably numbered less than a hundred over those ten years.

Highlights from two new poll workers' first day.

My experience was more like the fleshing out of a Norman Rockwell painting than it was disturbing in any way.

It was nearly freezing, and there was a steady rain, but the conversational tones never got heated, and the turnout for this election cycle was great. There was one exception. There was a solitary sixtyish year-old man who got bent out of shape when he realized we had three different color ballots. There were many people who had previously asked - "why the three different colors," but this guy sneered when he said it!

As I'd done a few times before, I explained that there were three different districts in our town and the color ballots corresponded to each district and their respective alderman candidates. He said nothing but stormed off.

My memories of this day will include the elderly woman who proudly showed off the loud blouse she'd bought on a whim last year. She finally had a special occasion to wear it. Not far behind her was another older woman who came in with a toy poodle who pranced around in all his finery. You'd think the way he was spinning around on his hind legs that he was the security detail for the event. BTW, there wasn't any except for him.

It was encouraging to see new voters there with their presumed parents - looking just a little nervous, but obviously proud to be doing the right thing. As is so often the case, the majority of the people there had been voting in that same building for decades, seeing their neighbors, the grocery store clerks, the folks from their churches, and the waitress from their favorite restaurant. And we can't forget the fireman.

I ran into one that I just might remember. I'd barely noticed the middle-aged guy approaching with his red jacket and town insignia. My line was growing, and I had just hunkered down trying to tear through some heavy-duty plastic around the next bundle of ballots when I noticed a large knife in my peripheral vision. He kindly offered to pierce through the plastic, and he helped us get moving again.

Though it might not be for everyone, I really enjoyed watching and interacting with people just being neighborly and doing what they think is best for our country. We hear about all the anger and division - "out there," but only one unhappy guy out of the six or seven hundred that I saw suggests that there's way less vitriol than we might expect.

And then there was the lady with the chewing gum.

She was having a great animated conversation with my wife only five feet away when she accidentally spit the wad of chewing gum out. It landed on my wife's hand and then plopped onto the ballot she was initialing. The woman was mortified, as she plunked the gum right back into her mouth. As it turns out, she "never" chews gum but had gotten some to hopefully help stifle a dry cough she'd just acquired. We reassured her it was no problem as she headed off to her booth.

In the process, we were gifted with an amusing visual to remind us of the fun day we had as poll workers.

CHAPTER 61

Stepping Back to Move Forward

Periodically, I find myself immersed in a conversation with a friend or acquaintance when I notice two different types of subtle changes in their demeanor. The first may be the wobbling of their upper body with closed eyes and almost a snoring sound. I take this to be a good sign - that maybe I have a soothing voice.

And then there's the other pattern I've noticed - maybe the twitching of their eyes, a little foam leaking between pursed lips or clenched fists pounding their thighs.

Though I'm obviously kidding, it is very important to stay in tune with the more subtle signals that listeners may send.

Take for instance, "George" - one of my friends here in the heartland. He's active in local causes, goes to the same UCC church, and we enjoy things like riding our motorcycles together. He even helped me attach the wings onto the ultralight I built a few years ago. And we do occasional bacon and eggs at the local diner but mainly just appreciate shooting the breeze.

Speaking of shooting, we're both gun owners. However, he worked for decades as an FBI agent, and I've worked for decades as a Physician Assistant doing lots of ER shifts. I've also worked in a couple of refugee camps. He's no doubt seen what bullets can do as have I, and yet we have different views on gun safety and a few other hot button topics.

A few months ago, we were having a nice, low-key discussion at a town park during a festival. Then the exchange of ideas drifted toward something political. Over the course of less than fifteen minutes, it became progressively more heated until suddenly George threw up his hands signaling "TIME OUT"!

He then followed up with - "I value our friendship too much to continue this conversation." With minimal reflection, I not only agreed but especially appreciated his mentally stepping back and establishing boundaries. This was a most valuable lesson for me.

Every conversation or transaction that we participate in has potential risks, benefits, and opportunity costs. We each have the option to grab the steering wheel when we see falling "rocks" ahead. How would things be different if every time we witnessed an interaction going sour, we merely stepped back and asked - "What's the most important thing to take away from this moment?

CHAPTER 62

Are We Enablers or Explorers

We are, in some sense, a part of every problem that we encounter.

We can be passive observers,

an enabler,

or, someone who gives their best to facilitate positive change.

We - get to Decide!

We are, in a similar way, a part of every problem that we face within.

We can be passive observers,

an enabler,

or we could be explorers who dig deeply and honestly to uncover the true obstacles that keep us from moving forward.

Every day, we get to decide.

CHAPTER 63

Moving Toward the Ties That Bind

Think for a moment about that single person you have connected with, more than anyone else. Now try to pin down what made you love that one individual above all others. Was it their looks, their kindness, their sense of humor, or their intelligence? I dare say your feelings went deeper than any of these.

What was it then that endeared you to that specific person? Was it that your thoughts and most sacred values resonated on a substantially deeper level?

The operative word that I'm zeroing in on here, is "deeper." The fibers that hold us together as humans are rarely on the surface, though to the casual observer they might appear to be. The Green Bay Packers T-shirt or that green and yellow hat may provide something in common to talk about.

Photography by Julius Drost - Unsplash

But dozens of memories shared about team triumphs will never come close to hitting the same spot as shared stories of being an unemployed single parent or fighting to survive – whether it's in combat or in a seriously abusive relationship. Experiences of common life challenges and stories of growth are readily available to connect human souls of every size, shape, and color.

The deeper the connection, the slower the rejection.

As I look back on the deteriorating relationships within my fold over the years, I must acknowledge that none of those relationships were well tended. Maintenance had become more challenging, and like a neglected garden, the weeds had overwhelmed the healthy growth of new life.

I can offer age old excuses that the time and energy were in short supply back then, but to be honest, it was more a case of my priorities. And who amongst us doesn't benefit from a periodic self-assessment of those?

The urgency of reversing the trends toward more divisiveness and resultant isolation cannot be overstated. We are obviously limited in what we can control, but we can at least minimize the chances that we're contributing to the larger problem. And at best, we can prioritize getting a better understanding of those beyond our usual circles.

I'm convinced that most people are decent and have respectable goals for themselves and their families. Very few would electively choose to step on their fellow humans without the constant prodding of others.

The filters through which we see and interpret life have changed. Those filters, all too often, distort truth, and in the process, convince us to focus on those areas where we disagree instead of those common values and priorities which unite us.

The trick is seeing past the exterior to the interior - where we are so very much the same.

EPILOGUE

It's Our Fingers that Turn the Dials

A Metaphor for Life

The above photograph is of my ultralight aircraft instrument panel. It is emblematic of the simplicity that defines the vehicle that I have chosen to escape the *complexities of life*. The latter would be more accurately depicted by a photo of a 747's instrument panel.

Regardless of the "ships" that you and I pilot, or their complexities, it is our fingers that turn the dials.

From the first flicker of our eyelids in the morning, we get to decide whether to let in more light or hold on to the darkness.

As the synapses explode with activity, we generate our first thoughts; we are the ones who get to dial in the focus, toward that which builds up or that which tears down. That which challenges or that which placates.

We get to spin the dial or turn it ever so deliberately - toward fluff or toward a higher purpose. To the right toward fear or the left toward trust.

Maybe there's a toggle switch . . . deal with that difficult conversation now *or* hope that the problem goes away "on its own." Flipping it either way is our choice, and ours alone.

Sometimes the dials get stuck or they just seem way too large to turn - for example - moving our sights from a sad past toward a more optimistic future. . . or from "I've always been this way," toward taking the first of twelve steps. Or maybe making the adjustment between mindlessly accepting and carefully discerning.

Or how about that enormous knob where we get to dial in how much we follow our peers versus follow our heart. That one is strategically located right next to the dial between cowardice and courage.

And then sometimes the problem is that the knobs have just gotten so slippery or seem to have a mind of their own - maybe spinning toward cruelty as we attempted to dial down tensions.

As the years race by, maybe we've relinquished more and more control to autopilot - finding it much easier than thoughtfully searching for the sweet spot between apathy and over-thinking, between charity and hedonism, or between gratitude and greed.

Every single day we get to deliberately adjust those dials or yield to the pressures of others around us. Accepting responsibility and then the secondary accountability doesn't necessarily make for a smoother flight, but it will increase the chances that we arrive at a more favorable destination.

AND Lastly . . .

Thank you all for joining me on this journey.

I encourage each one of you to

stretch beyond your comfort zone,

to get those conversations rolling,

and then savor the ride!

"The deeper the connection, the slower the rejection" - MVL

If you haven't already, please consider leaving a review for this book on Amazon – your support is greatly appreciated.

And for those who would like to follow along side as I make new encounters and connections, join me @ markvanlaeys.substack.com

NOTES: